Sunset

ADVENTURES IN FOOD

By the editorial staffs of Sunset Books and Sunset Magazine

Dorothy Krell, Cook Book Editor

Annabel Post, Home Economics Editor, Sunset Magazine

Helen Evans Brown, Sunset Magazine Food Consultant

Staff Home Economists: Jerry DiVecchio,

Beatrice Ojakangas, Chrisida Regnart, Karel Peer

Illustrations by Alice Harth

Sunset

Adventures in food

LANE BOOK COMPANY, MENLO PARK, CALIFORNIA

Library of Congress Catalog Card 64-22659
Title Number 201
First Edition
First Printing October 1964

Printed in the United States of America by A. Carlisle & Co.
Type Composition by Anderson, Ritchie & Simon
Binding by Cardoza Bookbinding Company

Foreword

To the good cook, every meal is a challenge and every dish that she attempts to make is looked upon as a work of art, an original creation that reflects her imaginative approach to cookery. It makes no difference whether she will serve it to a dozen or more admiring guests, or whether it will be for her family alone. In either case, it must live up to the standards of excellence set by any good cook. Its ingredients will be of the finest quality, its flavors will be blended to perfection, it will be cooked to just the right degree of doneness, and it will present an irresistible appearance when it is served.

The good cook is an adventuresome cook. She is receptive to new ideas, and she experiments—with seasonings, unusual ingredients, unfamiliar foods, new ways to serve familiar foods, interesting sauces.

Food adventure leads us to many parts of the world, and a good many foreign cultures are represented in this book. Some are simply new ways with foods that we serve often: from Scandinavia, green beans in an egg sauce; from Brittany, chicken roasted with a stuffing of small white onions. Some are seasoning tricks: lamb with dill, a bit of curry in scrambled eggs, a tarragon-flavored sauce for liver. Some introduce ingredients unfamiliar to many American cooks: dried chestnuts, litchi nuts, fresh bean sprouts. Still others are famous recipes: the Chicken Marengo created by Napoleon's chef; La Garbure, popular hearty soup of the Basques; Italy's *fettucine*. And a few, such as Costa Rica's *chirrasquillas*, or the *cous-cous* of North Africa, are exciting ventures into completely different worlds of cooking.

The recipes that follow have appeared in the Sunset Magazine feature, *Adventures in Food*. Helen Evans Brown, editor of this feature, has spent many years in the study of good and creative cooking. Her interest in the fascinating subject of food has taken her to many parts of the globe, and has led her to delve deeply into our own American cooking—particularly that of the West Coast where she lives. The recipes from this popular Sunset Magazine column are printed here in book form with the hope that they will lead many a reader into the exciting world of imaginative and adventuresome cookery.

Contents

Sunset

ADVENTURES IN FOOD

Appetizers & Hors d'Oeuvres

The versatility of hors d'oeuvres and appetizers is quite amazing. These tidbits are fascinating things both to the cook who creates them and to the guest who samples them. They fall into two distinct categories: the French *hors d'oeuvre*, which is fork food, served at the table to begin the meal; and the American version, generally finger food, served in the living room or on the patio with before-dinner drinks.

The French variety ranges from caviar and pâté to every conceivable meat, fish, or vegetable, simply but imaginatively sauced, and usually offered in variety. The morsels that we call "hors d'oeuvres" or "appetizers" for lack of a better name may also include caviar and pâté, and may, like the French hors d'oeuvres, be made from less expensive things as well. The primary requisite is that they be delightful in appearance and tantalizing in flavor.

This chapter includes some finger food, some French type hors d'oeuvres, a few outstanding dips (some hot, some cold), and one or two particularly savory spreads. We hope they'll inspire you to devise some fanciful combinations of your own.

Japanese Appetizers

These should be deep fried just before they are served, and they are so good it is worth the trouble.

Peel, clean, and grind ½ pound raw shrimp. Mix with ¼ cup finely chopped minced water chestnuts, 1 tablespoon finely minced green onion, 1 tablespoon soy, 1 unbeaten egg white, and 1 teaspoon grated ginger (fresh or candied). Trim crusts from 10 slices of bread, spread with the mixture, cut each slice in quarters. Just before serving, fry in deep fat until browned. Makes 40.

Osterreichische Eier

The name means "Eggs, Austrian Style." They are stuffed hard-cooked eggs that make an excellent appetizer or first course.

Shell 1 dozen hard-cooked eggs and cut in halves lengthwise. Remove yolks and mash with 1 raw egg yolk, 4 minced anchovies, ½ cup chopped cooked smoked tongue, 1 tablespoon vinegar, 1 tablespoon salad oil, and salt and pepper to taste. If the mixture still is not sufficiently soft, add a little more oil and vinegar or some mayonnaise. Stuff egg whites, piling high. Garnish each egg with a feather of parsley. Makes 2 dozen.

Camembert Spread

If you have often let a bit of Camembert or Brie or other really good cheese dry out simply because it was too small to serve, you'll appreciate this way of stretching small amounts. Make this spread while the cheese is still fresh, and it will be welcome next time you have a drop-in guest.

Peel the cheese and mash it, or if it is hard, grate it. Mix it with an equal amount of butter. For each ½ cup (or thereabouts) of this cheese-butter mixture, add 1 tablespoon bright red paprika (if you keep paprika in the refrigerator, it won't turn brown). Pack into jars, cover, and refrigerate. Before serving, mix in 1 tablespoon minced onion or chives for each ½ cup of the mixture. Spread on crisp crackers.

Shellfish Ravigote

Shellfish ravigote, served in scallop shells, if you have them, makes an elegant beginning for a dinner party.

Combine ½ teaspoon salt, a dash of cayenne, 3 tablespoons olive oil, 1 tablespoon wine vinegar, ½ teaspoon minced parsley, 1 chopped hard-cooked egg. Mix with 1 pound shrimp, lobster, or crab meat (use 2 cups canned or frozen shellfish if fresh is unavailable). Arrange in 6 to 8 scallop shells or other serving shells. Cover with green mayonnaise (below), and garnish each serving with an anchovy fillet. Makes 6 to 8 servings.

Green Mayonnaise: Put 8 sprigs watercress, 6 to 10 spinach leaves (depending on size), and 5 sprigs parsley in a bowl and cover with boiling water. Let stand for 6 minutes; drain and rinse in cold water. Put in the blender with 1¼ cups mayonnaise and 2 teaspoons lemon juice. Whirl until smooth and evenly colored.

Toasted coconut chips are good nibbling any time. To make them, remove meat from shell, peel off brown skin, and shave the meat in thin slices, using a potato peeler. Spread shavings on a cooky sheet and toast slowly in a moderately hot (375°) oven, turning occasionally, until crisp and lightly browned.

Vegetable Appetizers

These are especially good as warm-weather appetizers, but you'll find that they are welcome any time.

Try serving tiny canned beets, chilled, drained, and sprinkled lightly with lemon juice or tarragon vinegar; provide picks and sour cream for dunking. Raw asparagus is another delight; clean it well, cut off all the tough ends, and serve with a dip of mayonnaise, dill-flavored sour cream, or French dressing. Treat sweet onions this way: Peel and cut into ¼-inch slices, then soak in a mixture of 4 parts ice water to 1 part vinegar, seasoned with salt and oregano; drain, separate rings, and serve on ice.

Then there are the usual radishes, celery, cucumber slices, green pepper strips, and of course, carrots and cauliflower. Raw green beans and raw turnips are good, too.

Olive Pâté

Olive pâté with pumpernickel bread and radishes makes a distinguished appetizer.

Purée 3 cans (4 oz. each) minced ripe olives by forcing through a sieve or ricer. Mix with ¼ pound soft butter, 1 pressed garlic clove, a little freshly ground pepper, and ¼ teaspoon crushed fennel seeds (use a mortar and pestle). Mix well and serve on little plates with the thinly-sliced bread and the radishes cut in roses.

Cocktail Sandwiches

These tiny sandwiches, four from two slices of thin bread, are very good as appetizers. They can be made ahead and frozen.

Combine 1 cup minced turkey or chicken, 1 cup minced smoked tongue, ½ cup soft butter, and salt and prepared mustard to taste. Spread on slices of good white bread; top with slices of whole wheat bread, trim crusts, and cut in 4 squares or triangles. Spread is enough for 3 dozen tiny sandwiches.

Bagna Cauda

This robust appetizer dip is a fine beginning for an Italian meal. Make it in a small chafing dish, or, for an outdoor meal, in a saucepan over a charcoal fire.

Combine ½ pound butter, ½ cup olive oil, 4 to 8 puréed cloves of garlic (depending on your taste for garlic), and 2 cans (2 oz. each) anchovy fillets, chopped into small pieces. Heat gently for 10 minutes but do not allow to boil or brown. Serve piping hot, with an assortment of ice cold celery, carrot sticks, cauliflowerets, strips of green pepper, and raw green beans.

French-fried Mushrooms

For a hot appetizer that can be prepared ahead of time and cooked quickly at serving time, try French-fried mushrooms, cooked and served on long skewers.

Select 3 dozen uniform fresh mushrooms, preferably about 1 inch in diameter. Remove stems (save them for soup or sauces), and impale each cap on a long bamboo stick, inserting the point from edge to edge. Holding onto the ends of the sticks, swish caps through flour, then through seasoned beaten egg (mix together 2 eggs, 1 teaspoon salt, and a few grindings of pepper), then through fine cracker crumbs. Let dry while you heat deep fat to 360°. Fry mushrooms for 4 minutes, or until brown. Serve at once with this sauce: Combine ½ cup sour cream, ½ cup mayonnaise, 1 tablespoon minced dill pickles, 1 tablespoon chopped capers, and 1 minced fillet of anchovy.

Chili Almonds

This appetizer makes a hit with men.

Put 1 pound shelled unblanched almonds in a heavy pan with 1 tablespoon chili powder, 1 large clove crushed garlic, and ¼ cup butter or margarine. Cook over medium heat, stirring constantly, until crisp and lightly browned. Remove garlic, sprinkle nuts with coarse salt; cool before putting in jars.

Oysters and Sausages

A specialty of the Charente River region of France, this combination of hot, spicy sausages and cold, succulent oysters is sensational. It's filling, so if other appetizers are served, make them simple.

Serve oysters on the half shell, bedded on cracked ice. Nearby, have a chafing dish filled with piping hot, crispy pork sausages. The oysters and sausages are eaten together, for a contrast of flavors and temperatures.

Curried Almonds

Here's another simple appetizer, ideal to serve if the meal is to follow shortly. Serve these hot or cold.

Use blanched or unblanched almonds. To dry and crisp recently blanched almonds, spread them in a pan and bake in a slow oven (300°) for 20 to 30 minutes. Heat ¼ cup salad oil in a large frying pan. Add 2 pounds almonds; sprinkle them with 2 tablespoons fresh curry powder. Sauté, stirring, until nicely colored. Sprinkle with salt and drain on paper towels.

Chicken Wings in Soy

Here's an appetizer that is best served on the patio with large paper napkins, or better yet, with hot towels, for it is definitely a finger food.

Combine 1 cup each of soy, sherry, and water; add 1 crushed clove of garlic and 2 tablespoons grated fresh or crystallized ginger. Add 2 pounds chicken wings and simmer for 30 minutes, or until tender. Cool in the liquid and serve cold. Makes about 16 appetizers.

A good dip for chips or crackers is made by browning ½ cup sesame seeds in a heavy skillet, mixing them with an 8-ounce package of cream cheese, and seasoning the mixture with soy sauce. For variety, add chopped ginger, green onions, shrimps, clams, or chicken livers.

Garlic Cheese Fingers

Dry bread is best for these. Serve them with drinks, soups, or salads. They freeze very nicely.

Trim crusts from 4 slices of bread, and cut each slice into 4 strips, or fingers. Crush 1 clove garlic and heat with ¼ pound butter for 1 minute; discard garlic and brush bread sticks on all sides with the mixture. Roll in ½ cup of grated Parmesan or Romano cheese (or in sesame seeds or poppy seeds), and bake in a moderate oven (350°) for 15 minutes, or until nicely browned.

Hot Pepper Pecans

These are very simple to fix, and make excellent appetizers before an elaborate dinner.

For each cup of large pecan halves, melt 2 tablespoons butter in a shallow pan. Spread pecans evenly in one layer, and bake in a slow oven (300°) for 30 minutes, or until the nuts just begin to brown. Stir several times during the baking, and be sure not to overcook. Mix 2 teaspoons soy, ½ teaspoon salt, and 2 or 3 dashes liquid hot-pepper seasoning into the toasted nuts, turning them so the seasoning will be evenly distributed. Spread on a double thickness of paper towel to cool; pack in jars with tight-fitting lids.

Serving radishes with cheese is a Continental custom that we might well adopt. Select the smallest radishes possible, wash them well, snip off the roots and all but about ½ inch of the leaves, and arrange them on a board of assorted cheeses. Their crispness and peppery flavor is just right with almost any cheese.

Chopped Liver Appetizer

Served on lettuce and accompanied by thinly-sliced rye or pumpernickel bread, this makes a delicious first course.

Bake 1 pound calf's liver, preferably in one piece, in a moderately slow oven (325°) until your meat thermometer reads 150°, about 30 minutes. Do not season. Cool and remove skin and veins; chop meat with a sharp knife (do not grind it in the food chopper). Mince 6 green onions and cook until wilted in 2 tablespoons rendered chicken fat or butter, and mix with the liver. Chill. Just before serving, combine with another 2 tablespoons rendered chicken fat or butter, and season with salt. Makes about 1½ cups.

An Italian Appetizer

The combination of black olives and red tomatoes in this easy-to-make appetizer is very appealing.

Drain 1 can (7 oz., drained weight), jumbo pitted ripe olives and stuff each one with half a fillet of anchovy. (A 2-ounce can will just about do the job.) If you have any olives left over, fill them with a bit of almost anything: meat, nuts, cheese, smoked fish, celery. Or the fillings for these appetizers could be assorted. Put the olives in a bowl with 2 tablespoons olive oil, 1 puréed clove garlic, and ⅓ cup finely minced parsley. Mix well. Add a dozen or more stemmed cherry tomatoes, cover, and keep refrigerated until an hour before serving. Provide toothpicks to prevent oily fingers.

Chili con Queso

Here is a hot dip that has more distinction than most. There are many ways to make it, but this one is typical. Serve tostados (crisply fried tortillas) or crackers with this.

- ½ pound unsalted pork fat, cut into cubes
- 2 large cloves garlic, pressed
- 1 large onion, chopped
- 1 can (1 lb., 4 oz.) tomatoes
- 2 tablespoons flour
- ¼ cup undiluted evaporated milk
- 2 cans (4 oz. each) peeled green chilies
- About 1 teaspoon salt
- Liquid hot-pepper seasoning (optional)
- 1 pound coarsely shredded jack cheese

Sauté pork fat until brown and crispy; remove the pork from the fat, and reserve. Sauté garlic and onion in the fat until wilted. Add tomatoes, and cook until the liquid is reduced. Make a paste of the flour and milk, and stir in. Rinse chilies of their seeds, and chop. Combine with the tomato mixture; add salt to taste and a dash of liquid hot-pepper seasoning, if you want the mixture hotter. Pour the mixture into a chafing dish, add the pork cubes and the jack cheese, and serve as soon as the cheese is partially melted.

Charcoal-broiled Shrimp Appetizer

These are delicious, and the perfect appetizer to serve at a patio party while the meat is roasting.

Shell jumbo shrimp and split each deeply down the back, removing the sand vein. Insert a fillet of anchovy in each slit, wind with a half-slice of bacon (split bacon lengthwise), and fasten with a pick. Broil over charcoal until the bacon is crisp. Don't overcook if you want these at their best; they should be hot and juicy—never dry.

Broiled Shrimp with Vermouth

This is a mixture of French and Oriental cuisine. To make it completely Oriental, substitute sake for the vermouth.

Marinate 2 pounds shelled and deveined jumbo shrimp or prawns in ½ cup French-type (dry) vermouth, ¼ cup grated fresh ginger, 1 pressed clove garlic, and ¼ cup soy. Thread on skewers, brush with oil, and broil for 3 minutes on one side, 2 minutes on the other, brushing with the marinade during cooking.

Brandade de Morue

This famous dish from the south of France makes a lusty dip for chips or toast strips. It's also good served cold.

Cover 1 pound salt codfish with cold water and bring to a boil; drain. Repeat procedure, then cool the fish. Remove skin and bones; flake. Heat ¼ cup olive oil in top of double boiler; add 1 pressed clove of garlic and the fish. Cook over hot water for half an hour, stirring occasionally and thinning mixture as needed with heated milk (usually ½ to 1 cup milk). Remove from heat; whirl in blender or beat with an electric beater, gradually adding another ½ cup hot olive oil. Season to taste with salt and plenty of pepper, and serve from a chafing dish; or for an outdoor party, serve from a saucepan kept warm near the charcoal fire.

Smoked Salmon and Cheese Dip

Appetizer dips for potato chips or crackers, or for raw vegetables, are always popular. This one is exceptionally good, and a little different.

Combine 1 large package (8 oz.) softened cream cheese with ½ pint (1 cup) sour cream. Mix until smooth, adding a few drops of light cream if too thick (don't allow the mixture to become drippy). Stir in ¼ pound finely diced smoked salmon, 2 tablespoons finely chopped green onions, and 2 tablespoons chopped capers.

Try a little soy on avocado for a delicious first course. Soy's clean, salty flavor is just right with the rich creamy fruit.

Sables

Serve these cheese pastry triangles with beverages or to accompany soup or salad.

Combine ½ pound butter, ½ pound finely shredded sharp Cheddar cheese, 2¼ cups sifted flour, ¾ teaspoon salt, and a dash of cayenne. Mix well and chill. Roll ¼ inch thick, cut in small triangles, brush with slightly beaten egg, and bake in a moderate oven (350°) until lightly browned, about 8 minutes. Makes 6 to 8 dozen.

Brazil Nut Chips

These are irresistible as an appetizer, and they're also excellent as a topping for a casserole or scalloped dish, or to sprinkle on cooked green beans, asparagus, cauliflower, or other vegetables. Try them, too, on simply cooked fillet of sole.

Cover shelled Brazil nuts with boiling water and boil for 7 minutes. Drain, scrape off brown skin (it will come off easily), then cut lengthwise into thin slices. Spread out on a cooky sheet and dot with butter. Put in a moderate oven (350°) and bake until lightly browned, stirring occasionally. Drain on paper towels, then sprinkle lightly with salt.

Sicilian Antipasto

Serve this as the first course of an Italian dinner, with sliced salami, hard-cooked egg, and anchovies or sardines.

- 1 quart stuffed green olives
- 1 cup drained pickled capers
- 4 cups sliced celery
- 2 cups sliced onions, the slices cut in half if large
- ¼ cup finely slivered pickled red pepper
- 6 cloves peeled garlic, sliced very thin
- 1 cup olive oil
- ½ cup red wine vinegar
- 2 teaspoons salt
- 2 teaspoons whole fennel seed

Slice olives; add capers, celery, onions, red pepper, garlic, olive oil, wine vinegar, salt, and fennel seed. Mix well and let stand in the refrigerator for 24 hours, then pack tightly in jars, taking care to get some of the juices in each jar. If necessary, add olive oil to fill jars completely. Cover tightly and keep refrigerated. Makes about 4 pints.

A gay little appetizer is a stuffed radish. Make radish roses, cut out a bit of the center and fill with a mixture of 2 parts Roquefort or blue cheese, 1 part butter, and a little brandy or sherry.

Sardine Croûtes

These hot-from-the-broiler appetizers are unusual. They'll make a hit with party guests.

Drain 1 can (3½ or 4 oz.) boneless and skinless sardines and pound them in a mortar with ½ teaspoon anchovy paste, ½ teaspoon lemon juice, ½ teaspoon Worcestershire, a few grains of salt, and a dash of liquid hot-pepper seasoning. Mix with ¼ cup whipped cream (measured *after* it is whipped). Place by teaspoonfuls on small rounds of buttered toast and brown lightly under the broiler. Makes about 2 dozen.

Aguacates Rellenos

This recipe for *aguacates rellenos*, or stuffed avocados, is distinctly Mexican. It's especially good as the first course for a summer meal. Serve it with *tostados* (tortillas cut in wedges and fried crisp in shortening).

3 ripe avocados
1 large ripe tomato, peeled, seeded, and diced
1 tablespoon finely minced onion
1 teaspoon green chili sauce (or more if you want it hotter)
1 teaspoon salt
1 tablespoon olive oil
1 teaspoon lemon juice
2 teaspoons minced fresh coriander (or ½ teaspoon ground coriander)
Lettuce
Lemon wedges

Cut avocados in half, remove seeds, and carefully scoop out almost all the pulp, leaving only about a ¼-inch layer of it on the skins. Mash the avocado pulp and mix with diced tomato, minced onion, green chili sauce, salt, olive oil, lemon juice, and coriander. Fill avocado shells with this mixture, put on lettuce-lined plates, and garnish each plate with a wedge of lemon. Makes 6 servings.

Fried Ginger Pork

This Oriental way of preparing pork makes a wonderful appetizer to cook over the barbecue and serve while the steaks are grilling.

Cut 2 pounds boneless fresh pork shoulder in 1-inch cubes, and brown thoroughly on all sides in ¼ cup oil (sesame, peanut, or some other bland oil). Add 1 cup finely minced onion and 1 large clove garlic, pressed. Cook until the onion becomes soft, then add ½ cup soy, 1 tablespoon chopped fresh ginger, and 1 teaspoon sugar (or 1 tablespoon chopped preserved or crystallized ginger), and 2 tablespoons vinegar. Cover pan and let simmer for about 10 minutes, or until pork is done. Serve on toothpicks right from the pan.

Ginger Sausage Balls

Tiny ginger sausage balls make good appetizers. They may be frozen and reheated just before serving.

Mix 1½ pounds pure pork sausage meat with 1 very finely minced clove of garlic, 1 tablespoon grated fresh or candied ginger, and 3 egg yolks. Beat 3 egg whites and fold into the mixture. Drop by teaspoonfuls into hot deep fat (370°) and fry until brown and pork is thoroughly done, about 5 minutes. Drain on paper towels and serve hot. Makes 36 to 40 appetizers.

Boeuf Toscany

The popularity of Beef Tartare has led cooks to further adventures with raw beef. One is this raw beef appetizer, Boeuf Toscany.

Have 1 pound of lean beef (tenderloin, rump, or sirloin) sliced thin. Marinate it in ¼ cup olive oil, 2 tablespoons lemon juice, 1 teaspoon finely minced fresh rosemary, 1 clove garlic crushed in 1 teaspoon salt, and ¼ teaspoon freshly ground black pepper. Allow to stand in the refrigerator for an hour or more, then sprinkle with finely minced parsley, and serve with buttered pumpernickel bread.

If you serve a pâté or other rich mixture as an appetizer, also serve something light—crisp raw celery and other raw vegetables, or slices of cherry tomatoes laid on tiny rounds of thinly-sliced buttered bread.

Turkey Appetizers

If you have leftover turkey, you can use it to make this delicious, simple appetizer. Wrap the meat—either white or dark—in freezer paper and freeze until it is needed. Then thaw enough to cut in neat cubes.

Mix 1 cup mayonnaise with 1 teaspoon soy and 1 tablespoon grated fresh or candied ginger, or 2 teaspoons curry powder. Roll turkey cubes in this mixture, covering them on all sides, then roll in chopped, toasted, blanched almonds. Impale on wooden picks and chill until serving time.

Croûtes Suisse

Croûtes Suisse (Swiss crusts) are a nice hot hors d'oeuvre to start off a meal. They can be made ahead and baked at the last minute.

Cut thin slices of bread into rounds to fit the bottoms of 6 buttered individual baking dishes. Saturate bread with a dry white table wine (about 1 tablespoon for each bread slice). Make a sauce of 4 tablespoons each butter and flour and 2 cups milk. Stir gradually into 3 slightly beaten egg yolks. Add 1 cup shredded Swiss cheese, a few grains cayenne, and ¾ teaspoon salt. Divide among the 6 dishes, and bake in a hot oven (400°) until bubbly brown.

When serving such rich drinks as Tom and Jerrys and eggnogs, the wise hostess will keep the appetizers as simple as possible. Small, toasted cheese sandwiches, or dainty sandwiches of lettuce or watercress, or crisp hot buttered toast are good choices. If you do serve cookies or cakes, don't frost them. Fruit cake and elaborate petits fours should be kept for desserts, or for afternoon tea.

Mushrooms Bourguignonne

Just as *Bordelaise* pertains to Bordeaux, *Bourguignonne* refers to the Burgundy region of France. It usually means the dish is cooked with red Burgundy wine. Here are mushrooms cooked in the Burgundian manner, and good not only as an appetizer, but also as a garnish with roast beef or to glorify hamburgers. To serve them as an appetizer, you can prepare them in an electric frying pan, if you wish, and serve them speared on toothpicks.

Clean 1 pound medium-sized fresh mushrooms and remove stems (save for soups and sauces). Put mushroom caps in frying pan with 1 cup red Burgundy or Pinot Noir, 1 tablespoon minced shallots or green onions, 1 tablespoon minced parsley, 1 crushed clove garlic, ¼ cup butter, ¼ teaspoon salt, and a few grindings of black pepper. Cook for 6 or 7 minutes, or until the mushrooms are tender. Discard garlic before serving.

Cheese Paprikas

Serve these savory little snacks as appetizers or to accompany soups, salads, iced tea or coffee, or a glass of wine. If you want them extra fancy, brush with beaten egg and sprinkle with cheese, chopped nuts, or sesame seed before baking.

½ cup grated almonds or filberts (whirl them in a blender or use a nut grater)
¾ cup butter
1½ cups sifted flour
¾ cup grated Parmesan cheese
1 tablespoon fresh paprika
1 teaspoon salt
1 whole egg
1 egg yolk

Combine grated almonds or filberts with other ingredients. Mix with your hands until completely blended and pliable. Form into 1 or 2 rolls 1½ inches in diameter and wrap in waxed paper or clear plastic film. Chill. To serve, cut in ¼-inch slices, and arrange on an ungreased cooky sheet; bake in a moderately slow oven (325°) for about 12 minutes. Makes about 6 dozen.

Hummus Bethaine

Next time you want to serve something a little different in the way of an appetizer, try this one that is very popular in Arab countries. This is an easy version, using canned garbanzos.

Drain 1 can (15 or 16 oz.) garbanzos, but save the liquid. Put in a blender (or purée) with 1 peeled clove of garlic, 2 tablespoons sesame oil (the toasted brownish kind, available in Oriental markets), and 2 tablespoons toasted sesame seeds (brown them, stirring, in a heavy skillet). Blend smooth, adding as much of the garbanzo liquid as necessary to make a smooth paste, like not-too-stiff mashed potatoes. Add salt and lemon juice to taste, put in a mound on a dish, and sprinkle with minced parsley. (You may also pour a little olive oil over all, if you want to be very authentic.) Garnish with whole cooked garbanzos, if you have them, and serve with Syrian cracker bread, or the Syrian-type sesame cracker now in many markets.

Mushrooms Provençale

Stuffed mushrooms are popular as an appetizer. Here is one good way to prepare them.

Select 1 pound of uniform-sized mushrooms about 1¼ inches in diameter. Cook in ¼ cup olive oil, along with 2 crushed cloves garlic, for 4 minutes. Cool and remove stems. Reserve caps. Chop stems and mix with ¼ cup minced chives, ½ cup bread crumbs, 1 can (2 oz.) drained chopped anchovies, and the juices left in the sauté pan. Stuff mushroom caps with the mixture. Just before serving, slip the pan of stuffed mushrooms under the broiler to heat and brown slightly.

Quiche de Crabe

This makes a superb hors d'oeuvre. Make it with fresh crab, if you can get it, otherwise, use canned or frozen crab meat. This is also good as a luncheon or supper main dish.

Line a 9-inch pie pan with pastry, preferably one made with part (or all) butter. Flute the edge nicely and brush the inside with an egg white that has been lightly beaten. Let dry. Sauté 2 tablespoons minced shallots or green onions in 1 tablespoon butter until wilted. Mix with 1 pound shredded fresh crab meat or 2 cans (6½ oz. each) crab meat. Sprinkle with 1 tablespoon flour. Shred ¼ pound Swiss cheese and sprinkle half of it in the pie shell. Spread the crab meat over that, then sprinkle the remaining cheese over the top. Mix 3 beaten eggs, 1 cup light cream, ½ teaspoon salt, a couple of gratings of pepper, and a little freshly grated nutmeg. Pour this into the pie, put in a hot oven (400°), and bake for 10 minutes. Reduce heat to 350° and continue baking for about 40 minutes, or until a knife inserted in the center comes out clean. Serve warm (though it's good cold, too). Makes 6 servings.

Blinis

Among the most elegant appetizers you can serve are blinis, yet this sophisticated dish can star at the most informal of parties, with the little yeast buckwheat cakes being cooked at the table (or on the patio). This easy recipe calls for buckwheat pancake mix rather than the harder-to-find buckwheat flour. It makes enough for 8 people.

About 1½ hours before serving time, soften 1 package yeast (active dry or compressed) in ½ cup warm water. Beat together 2 cups buckwheat pancake mix, 1 cup hot water, 1 cup milk, 2 eggs, and 3 tablespoons melted butter. Add the yeast mixture and let rise until light (about 1½ hours). To serve, drop the batter by small spoonfuls (the blinis should be 2½ or 3 inches in diameter) onto a hot griddle; cook until brown on one side, and turn and brown the other side. Pass your guests a couple of blinis at a time on a hot plate, and let them spoon on caviar or some other filling, some melted butter, and sour cream.

For the filling, serve icy cold red caviar (to keep the caviar very cold, you can nest its bowl in crushed ice), or one of these other fillings: smoked salmon, thinly sliced and not too cold; hard-cooked eggs, chopped and mixed with enough melted butter to bind; flaked finnan haddie; smoked Alaska cod; or smoked sturgeon.

A talmouse originally was a pastry shell filled with a mixture containing either cheese or frangipani. The pastry was cut in circles, the filling put in the middle, and the edges turned up over it to form a tricorn similar to a pope's cap, or talmouse. The shape is the same as hamantaschen, that delicious Jewish poppy seed pastry. Why not make little appetizers in the same shape? They can be filled with any fish, meat, or cheese mixture.

Special Avocado Cocktail

Here's a refreshing way to begin a dinner.

Make a sauce by combining ½ cup mayonnaise, ½ cup heavy cream, whipped, 1 teaspoon lemon juice, and 2 ounces caviar. Serve over diced avocado arranged in cocktail glasses. A small leaf of lettuce can garnish each serving. Makes 6 to 8 servings.

Gougère

This wonderful concoction of *choux* paste and Swiss cheese must be served hot from the oven. This is a Burgundian recipe. Try it as an appetizer, first course, or with a salad and a glass of wine for lunch.

¼ cup butter
½ cup milk
½ cup flour
2 eggs
¾ cup finely diced Swiss cheese

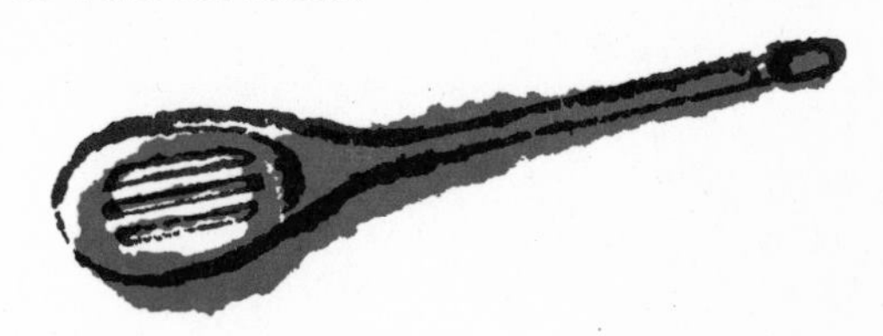

Grease a large cooky sheet and mark an 8 or 8½-inch circle on it. To make the choux paste (cream puff base), cook butter with milk until the butter is melted, then stir in flour all at once. Stir over heat until the mixture leaves the sides of the pan and forms a ball. Cool slightly; then beat in eggs and ¼ cup of the cheese. Spread on the cooky sheet in the circle already marked. Sprinkle with the remaining ½ cup of the cheese, and bake in a moderate oven (350°) for 30 minutes, or until billowy brown. Cut in wedges like a pie and serve immediately.

This will serve 4 for lunch, more as an appetizer. For a party, double this recipe and spread it on a 12 by 15-inch cooky sheet, and bake in the same way; then cut into 1½-inch squares. This will make 80 appetizers.

Liptauer

In Austria, this spread usually accompanies beer and dark bread. It makes a fine appetizer, especially if you give each guest a small plate and let him mix his own combinations, using some of the cheese mixture and as many of the accompaniments as meet his fancy.

For about 3 cups spread, combine 2 large packages (8 oz. each) cream cheese with ¼ cup sweet butter and 2 tablespoons heavy cream. Whip until fluffy, and shape into a mound on a decorative dish. Surround with small dishes of chopped onion, chopped anchovy fillets, capers, and chopped chives. Also have a large bowl of radish roses on hand, and some thinly-sliced rye bread.

Shrimp on a Stick

Skewered shrimp, cooked right at the cocktail table in an electric frying pan or other table cooker, makes a dramatic appetizer.

- 2 pounds raw jumbo shrimp or prawns (16 to 24), shelled and de-veined
- 2 cups white wine
- 6 cups water
- ¼ cup white wine vinegar
- 1 onion, sliced
- 1 carrot, sliced
- 1 tablespoon salt
- 2 whole cloves
- 1 stalk celery, sliced
- Herb bouquet (bay, parsley, thyme)
- Dill butter (below)

Thread each shrimp on a long thin bamboo skewer. Insert point of skewer at tail of shrimp and impale its full length, so that the point of the skewer just shows at the head end of the shrimp. Refrigerate until cooking time. Make a court bouillon of the wine, water, wine vinegar, onion, carrot, salt, cloves, celery, and herb bouquet. Bring to a boil, turn to a simmer, and cook for ½ hour. Strain.

When guests have assembled, bring the court bouillon to a boil, pour into the frying pan or other table cooker which has been placed on the cocktail table. Bring threaded shrimp, attractively arranged on a platter, and give each guest a napkin, a dish of prepared Dill Butter (see below), and a small tray or plate. When the court bouillon is bubbling, add one skewer of shrimp for each guest, allowing the handles to stick out but completely immersing the shellfish. Cook for about 5 minutes, or until they have lost their translucent look. Serve one to each guest, to be dipped in the Dill Butter and eaten right from the skewer. Cook remaining shrimp in one or two batches. This is a generous amount for 8 persons.

Dill Butter: Cream together ½ pound soft butter, 1 tablespoon minced fresh dill or 2 teaspoons dill weed, 1 teaspoon lemon juice, and a dash of liquid hot-pepper seasoning. (Or use 1 or 2 teaspoons curry powder or a crushed clove of garlic instead of the dill weed.) Divide this among small dishes or saucers, one for each guest. Serve at room temperature.

Soups

To count the varieties of soups would be like counting the stars on a cloudless night. There are elegant soups, meticulously simmered, seasoned, and clarified by master chefs, or lowly ones that bubble on peasant stoves and into which go trimmings of meat, poultry, and vegetables to add their flavors to the savory brew. There are consommés and cream soups, bisques and purées, and the many hearty soups that are the mainstay of the poor in many countries and the delight of epicures at home.

Then there are the cold soups. Although jellied consommé has been known for many years, it is only recently that cold soups have come into their own in America. When they did appear, they were taken up with enthusiasm, and chefs and home cooks began to devise cold soups of their own and to search the culinary lore of other countries for Old World favorites that would tantalize our American palates.

Many of the soups in this chapter are adaptations of famous foreign soups; others are new and unusual, but seasoned with skill and inspiration, and deserving of as much praise as the famous ones.

Semi-quick Borscht

There are many different versions of borscht, the most complicated made with a fermentation of beets and/or cabbage, and the simplest made by combining canned consommé and beet juice. This recipe falls somewhere between. It is hearty enough to make a meal. You can strain it, if you wish, and serve it either hot or cold.

Cover 3 pounds meaty beef shanks with 2 quarts water and bring to a boil. Skim, cover, and simmer for 1 hour. Add another 1 quart water, a large can (1 lb., 13 oz.) tomatoes, a large can (1 lb., 11 oz.) sauerkraut, 2 chopped onions, and 2 teaspoons sugar. Continue cooking for another hour. Remove meat from bones, dice it, and return it to the pot. Add salt and pepper to taste and a little more sugar if needed; cook for another 10 minutes. Serve from a tureen and pass a bowl of cold sour cream. Makes 8 servings.

Browned whipped cream makes an attractive topping for many soups. Try it on cream of tomato, pea, celery, or any other creamed soup. Put heated soup in individual pots or bowls, top each with about 2 tablespoons whipped cream, and put under the broiler for 2 or 3 minutes to brown.

Chinese Chicken Soup

A Chinese soup that is the very quintessence of chicken flavor may be made with inexpensive chicken backs, obtainable at poultry markets that sell chicken parts.

Cover 4 pounds of chicken backs and 1 chicken breast with 6 cups cold water, and simmer slowly. Remove the breast as soon as it is tender (after about 10 minutes), and continue cooking the backs, adding more water if necessary, until all the flavor is extracted.

Strain off stock; discard chicken backs. Slice the chicken breast fine; also slice ½ pound fresh mushrooms, through stems and all; cut 1 large canned bamboo shoot in thin pieces; slice 3 green onions and half of the tops on the diagonal. Add these ingredients to the stock, season with 2 tablespoons sherry, and add soy or salt to taste. Simmer for 3 minutes. Makes 6 servings.

Hungarian Iced Tomato Soup

Fresh tomatoes are used to make this delightfully refreshing and appetizing-looking cold soup.

Peel 2 pounds ripe red tomatoes, chop, and heat with 3 cups dry white table wine (part or all may be chicken stock, but the recipe won't be Hungarian). Strain and season with 1½ teaspoons salt and just enough sugar to reduce acidity, about 1 tablespoon—it shouldn't be sweet. Chill well and pour into 6 or 8 bouillon cups or small glass bowls. Top each with a spoonful of slightly sweetened whipped cream.

Lady Curzon Soup

Here's a good soup for your "quick tricks" file. It calls for turtle soup, but it's also very good when made with beef bouillon or oxtail soup.

For every 2 servings, cook 1 teaspoon curry powder in 1 tablespoon butter for 2 minutes. Add 1 can (10 oz.) turtle soup (or beef bouillon or oxtail soup), bring to a boil, remove from the heat, and mix into 1 beaten egg yolk. Add ¼ cup sherry and pour into bowls. Top with whipped cream. If desired, the soup may be poured into heat-proof bowls and put under the broiler to brown the whipped cream lightly before serving.

Straciatella

Italian bread sticks are a good accompaniment to Straciatella, a rich Italian broth with flecks of egg.

Bring to simmering point (do not boil) 2 quarts of well-seasoned beef or chicken broth. Beat 3 eggs until thick; add 2½ tablespoons farina, ¼ cup grated Parmesan cheese, a few grains of salt, and a little grated nutmeg. Add 2 tablespoons of the simmering broth to the egg mixture, and beat thoroughly. Pour this into the soup, whisking constantly with the other hand. Simmer for 2 minutes more. Makes 8 servings.

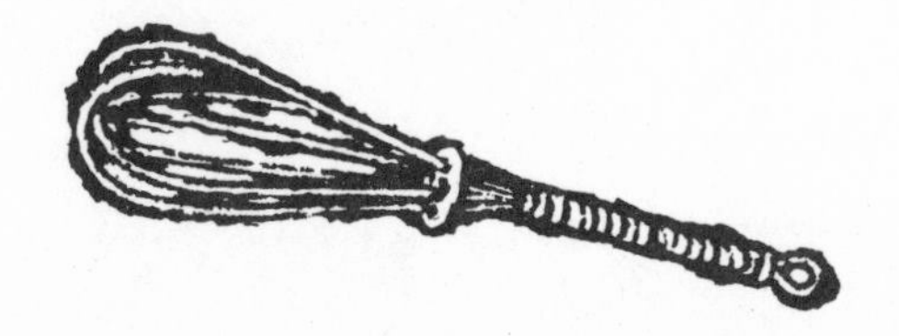

Cheese Soup

Serve this rich soup either hot or cold.

Simmer 6 pounds of chicken backs in 2 quarts water for 3 hours, adding water if needed to keep covered. Strain; discard bones. Boil the strained stock until it is reduced to 1 cup. Cook 1 chopped onion in 2 tablespoons butter until soft. Blend in ¼ cup flour, 1 puréed clove garlic, and ⅛ teaspoon ground cumin seed; gradually stir in the chicken stock and 1 quart milk. Simmer, stirring occasionally, until thick. Add 2 cups aged Cheddar cheese, shredded; stir until melted. Taste; add salt, pepper, and more cumin if you wish. To serve hot, garnish with croutons; to serve cold, garnish with shreds of the same cheese. Makes 6 servings.

Rice Soup

Here's a soup that is wonderfully smooth and creamy and can be flavored in dozens of ways. This is a true adventure in cooking, for the soup you make will be your own.

Cook ½ cup rice in 1½ quarts chicken or turkey stock until it is a mush. Force through a sieve or whirl smooth in a blender. Add 1 cup cream (light or heavy, as you wish) and reheat. At this point, choose your seasoning: mixed herbs, garlic, curry, chili powder, your favorite blended seasoning, puréed sorrel, deviled ham, puréed cooked chicken livers, grated cheese, artichoke or pimiento purée, or just plain salt and pepper. Add these to taste. Now, beat 1 egg yolk, mix with 1 cup of the hot soup, and stir gradually into the remainder. Heat, but do not boil. Serve at once with croutons or with a suitable garnish: diced avocado, chopped chutney, slivered almonds, chopped chives, crumbled crisp bacon, ham cubes, anything that appeals to you. Makes 6 servings.

La Garbure

This famous soup is the mainstay of the Basques. There are several different versions, and each cook has his own variation. Basically, it's a thick vegetable stew, with bacon and sausage. In the Basque country, *confits d'oie* (preserved goose) or *confits de porc* (preserved pork) is used in place of sausage. The Basques make the soup in an earthenware casserole called a *toupin*, but any heavy pan will do.

- ½-pound piece bacon
- 4 quarts water
- 1 pound potatoes, peeled and cut in chunks
- 2 bunches leeks, sliced
- 1 bunch turnips, cut in chunks
- 2 or 3 onions, peeled and cut in chunks
- 1 bunch large carrots, scraped and sliced
- 2 cups fresh or frozen peas
- 2 cups dried beans soaked overnight, or frozen lima beans
- 1 tablespoon salt
- ¾ pound peeled Spanish-style sausages (chorizo)
- 1 small cabbage, sliced
- 2 or 3 red or green peppers, chopped

Put bacon in pan, add the water, and bring to a boil. Add potatoes, leeks, turnips, onions, carrots, peas, and beans. Bring to a boil, turn heat low, add salt, and simmer until the vegetables are soft, adding water if necessary.

Add sausages, cabbage, and peppers. Continue cooking, stirring occasionally, until the potage is very thick and the vegetables are soft. Fish out bacon, cut in slices, and return to the pot. Correct the seasoning, and serve with red wine. (In the Basque country, the peasants like to eat the solid part of the garbure, then add a glass of red wine to what soup is left in their plates.) This very hearty dish will serve 8 to 10.

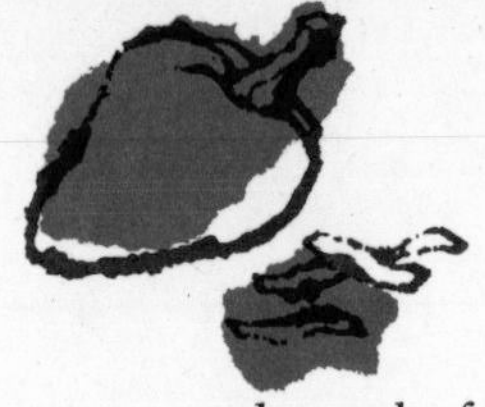

Iced Pimiento Soup

Here's an unusual chilled soup. It's easy to make, colorful, and very refreshing.

Press the contents of 1 can (4 oz.) pimientos through a food mill, and combine with 2 tablespoons scraped onion and 2 cups light cream (or whirl ingredients in a blender). Bring to a simmer, add salt if needed, and chill. Combine with 2 cans (10½ oz. each) jellied consommé, and serve very cold, topped with bits of pimiento. Makes 6 to 8 servings.

Billi Bi

The soup called Billi Bi, now popular in elegant restaurants, is a rich concoction made with mussels, white wine, and cream. It may be served either hot or cold. However, since mussels are not always obtainable, we have substituted clams so you can enjoy this soup all year round. You use only the broth from the clams. Use the clams themselves for another meal—chilled and dressed with mayonnaise or vinaigrette sauce, or chopped and mixed with cream cheese as a sandwich filling.

- 3 dozen medium-sized clams
- 4 large shallots or green onions, chopped
- 1 large onion, chopped
- 1½ cups white wine
- 1 tablespoon chopped parsley
- Freshly ground pepper (about 3 turns of the mill)
- Liquid hot-pepper seasoning
- 3 cups heavy cream
- 2 egg yolks, beaten
- Salt to taste
- Paprika

Scrub clams and put in a heavy pan with shallots, onion, wine, parsley, pepper, and a dash of liquid hot-pepper seasoning. Cover and put over heat. Let simmer for 20 minutes. Strain to remove clams, then strain the stock again through several layers of cheesecloth. Reheat broth, then add cream and continue heating; just before it boils, very gradually stir 1 cup of the hot liquid into the beaten egg yolks. Stir egg mixture back into liquid in pot, return to low heat, and cook, stirring, just long enough to thicken slightly. (Do not boil.) Correct seasoning, adding salt as necessary. Serve hot or chilled. Garnish each cup with a dash of paprika. Makes 6 servings.

Artichoke Soup

This very fine soup can be made quickly and easily with frozen artichoke hearts. It's good either chilled or hot.

Cook 1 package (9 oz.) frozen artichoke hearts in 2 cups chicken stock until tender; force them through a sieve or whirl in a blender; add milk or cream until thinned to the desired consistency, and season with salt and pepper to taste. Makes 4 servings.

Many hostesses find that serving soup in the living room simplifies a guest dinner. The table may be set for the main course; and serving the soup is a nice way to get across the idea that it's time to dine. Have the soup in a tureen, and ladle it into bouillon cups.

Purée Cressonière

A really good, rich soup is a meal in itself, if it's accompanied by some special hot bread—fresh rolls, popovers, cornbread sticks, or homemade bread. And this French cress and potato soup is a particularly good nomination.

- 2 bunches watercress
- 2 large leeks
- 2 large potatoes, peeled and diced
- 1½ quarts seasoned chicken stock
- 2 tablespoons butter
- 2 tablespoons flour
- 2 egg yolks
- ¾ cup light cream

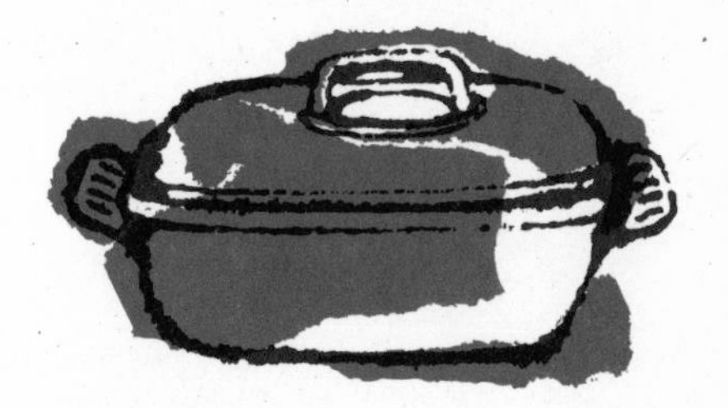

Discard the tough stems of watercress. Reserve 1 cup of the leaves; chop the remainder. Split leeks, wash thoroughly, discard tough green part, and chop. Combine chopped watercress, leeks, and potatoes, and cook in the chicken stock until tender. Force through a strainer or whirl in a blender (you'll have to do the latter in 2 or 3 batches), then return to the pot and reheat. Mix together butter and flour, and add to soup; stir over heat until thickened. Beat egg yolks with cream, and beat into soup. Correct seasoning and pour into a heated soup tureen. Garnish the top with the reserved leaves of cress. Makes about 6 servings.

Menlo Cream of Clam Soup

This is a distant cousin of Boula—a soup made by combining turtle soup and purée of fresh peas and served with a topping of browned whipped cream. It's easy to make and very popular.

Put 1 can (7 oz.) undrained minced clams in the blender with 1 cup heavy cream. Add the merest suspicion of puréed garlic (about ¼ of a small clove, pressed, or as much as you can pick up with the flat side of a toothpick). Also add 1 teaspoon *glacé de viande* (see page 154), if you have it, or 1 teaspoon Worcestershire. Whirl smooth in the blender.

Cook 1 tablespoon flour and 1 tablespoon butter together for 2 minutes; gradually stir in 1 cup bottled clam juice and 1 cup milk. Combine with clam mixture and simmer until slightly thickened and smooth. Correct seasoning, pour into 3 or 4 heat-proof bowls, and top with ¾ cup heavy cream, whipped. Put under the broiler to brown lightly. Serve immediately. Makes 3 or 4 servings.

Clam Chowder

Here is a basic chowder recipe you can embellish. Your personal touch could be adding a little curry powder, dill weed, minced parsley, thyme, or whatever your fancy dictates. You won't need salt; in fact you may need to add a bit of milk if the soup is too salty.

1 pound potatoes
1 cup water
½ cup (about 3 oz.) finely diced salt pork
1 medium-sized onion, chopped
½ pint (1 cup) bottled clam juice
1 can (8 oz.) minced clams, undrained
1 cup heavy cream
Freshly ground white pepper or liquid hot-pepper seasoning

Peel, cut, and finely dice potatoes; put in a pan with the water, cover, and cook until just tender. Meanwhile, cook salt pork until crisp; remove from pan with a slotted spoon and reserve. In the same fat, cook onion until golden; drain. Combine ingredients, add clam juice, clams, and cream. Add a dash of freshly ground white pepper or a dash of liquid hot-pepper seasoning, and whatever other seasoning you like. Pour soup into a heated tureen and serve with pilot biscuits or hot homemade bread. Makes about 2 quarts.

Vegetables

A truly good cook takes as much joy in discovering an exciting way to serve spinach as she does in whipping up a new dessert. It is easy today to serve a *variety* of vegetables, for fast transportation and constantly improving techniques in freezing have made most vegetables available throughout the year. But the good cook looks for more than variety in the *kind* of vegetable she serves. She looks, too, for new and interesting ways to vary *each* vegetable. For the most part, vegetables cooked lightly and sauced simply with butter will be at their best, but there are many variations on this basic theme: lime juice to give a lift to green beans; beets cooked with apples and lightly seasoned with nutmeg; carrots with the delightfully compatible flavor of caraway.

Increased interest in foreign foods and foreign ways of cooking both unusual vegetables and the more familiar ones has contributed even more variety to vegetable cookery. The Scandinavians season beans with a dill-flavored cream sauce; the Mexicans cook bananas in a crisp batter and serve them as a vegetable; a Flemish way with carrots turns them into dinner party fare. The knowing cook will give vegetables the extra attention they deserve—and maybe even feature a perfectly prepared vegetable as a separate course as the French often do.

Green Beans Polonaise

Use small tender green beans for this attractive vegetable dish.

For each pound of beans, have ready the sieved yolk of 1 hard-cooked egg and 2 tablespoons fresh bread crumbs (you can whirl sliced bread in a blender). Leave the beans whole, but remove the tips, and cook in salted water until just tender but still bright green and crisp. Drain and arrange on a dish neatly, as you would asparagus stalks; keep beans hot. Quickly brown bread crumbs in 3 tablespoons butter. Pour sizzling hot over the beans; sprinkle with the sieved egg yolk, and serve at once. Makes 3 or 4 servings.

Green Beans in Egg Sauce

This is a Scandinavian way with beans, and a delicious one. It's a good vegetable dish to serve with simply broiled fish or with lamb chops.

Slice 2 pounds tender green beans on the diagonal and cook until tender. Drain and mix with the following sauce before serving: Make a roux with 3 tablespoons each butter and flour. Add 2 teaspoons dill weed (or even better, fresh dill, if you can find it). Blend in 2 cups milk. Cook, stirring, until thickened, then season with salt and pepper and simmer for 5 minutes. Beat 2 egg yolks into ¼ cup light cream, then add a little of the hot sauce. Stir into the remainder of the sauce, add 1 teaspoon lemon juice, and heat gently but do not boil. Makes 6 servings.

Green Beans with Lime Juice

Here's an interesting way to prepare green beans, fresh, frozen, or canned.

Cook fresh or frozen beans until almost tender. Drain cooked or canned beans well and cut into small pieces (smaller than "cut green beans"). For each 2 cups beans, melt 2 tablespoons butter in a heavy frying pan. Add the beans, 2 tablespoons minced parsley, and salt and pepper to taste. Cook, stirring, for 5 minutes. Add 1 tablespoon lime juice, mix well, and serve at once.

Huevos con Platano

Bananas prepared in this Mexican way are served as a vegetable. They are delicious with fried or charcoal-broiled chicken. (With a sauce of melted currant jelly, they become a delicious dessert, but substitute butter for the salad oil when you cook them.)

Peel and split 3 bananas lengthwise, and cut each piece in half. Dip in lemon juice. Make this batter: Separate 4 eggs and beat yolks until thick and light. Add ¼ cup flour and ½ teaspoon salt. Beat the egg whites until stiff but not dry, and fold into yolks. Drop the drained banana pieces into the batter, one at a time. Pick up with a spoon and slide into a large skillet with plenty of moderately hot oil, part of which may be olive oil. Turn almost at once, then cook until brown on both sides. Drain on paper towels. Makes 6 servings.

For a simple dressing for green beans, add 1 ounce of chipped beef, broken into pieces, to 1 cup of thin cream sauce, and heat. This is enough to dress 1 pound of beans.

Garbanzo Bean Casserole

Greek flavors are apparent in this quick casserole. It would be a good dish to include on a buffet featuring baked ham.

- 2 cans (1 lb. each) undrained garbanzo beans
- 1 cup chopped onion
- 1 teaspoon crushed rosemary
- 3 tablespoons minced parsley
- 1 can (1 lb.) tomatoes, drained and chopped
- Salt and pepper to taste
- 2 whole cloves garlic
- ½ cup olive oil

Combine garbanzos with onion, rosemary, parsley, tomatoes, and salt and pepper to taste. Sauté garlic in olive oil until lightly browned; discard garlic and stir oil into the bean mixture. Turn into a 2½-quart casserole and bake in a moderate oven (350°) for 1 hour. Makes 8 servings.

Frijoles Refritos

In Mexico, *frijoles refritos*, or refried beans, are served morning, noon, and night. When properly cooked, they are indeed delicious and go nicely with many charcoal-broiled meats, as well as with Mexican foods. They are rather tedious to prepare, because they require long, slow cooking and considerable mashing. But they freeze beautifully, so you can make enough for several meals. The secret of good frijoles, we believe, is plenty of lard and/or bacon drippings. The Mexicans use either or both.

For a large amount of *frijoles refritos* (enough for about 30 servings), cover 4 pounds (9 cups) Mexican pink or red beans or pintos with 6 quarts warm water, and cook until tender. This usually takes about 2 hours, but beans differ in dryness and hardness. Add 1 tablespoon salt after the beans are tender. Drain, but save the liquid.

Melt 1 pound (2 cups) lard or bacon drippings in a large, heavy pot (a Mexican earthenware *cazuela* is ideal). Add 2 cups beans and mash them with a potato masher until smooth. Add some bean liquid, then more beans. Mash as before, repeating until all the beans and liquid have been used. Cook slowly, stirring occasionally, until of the desired thickness, then add 1 more cup lard or bacon drippings, and continue cooking until the beans dry out slightly.

As beans thicken, they are more apt to stick, so stir often and add even more lard if you like. More salt will probably be needed, but the exact amount depends on what kind of fat you use. Cool, divide in desired portions, package, and freeze.

Beets Béarnaise

The lowly beet becomes an epicurean treat when prepared this way.

2 pounds beets
2 tablespoons tarragon vinegar
½ cup (¼ pound) butter
¼ teaspoon dry mustard
2 chopped shallots or green onions
¼ teaspoon tarragon
¼ teaspoon salt
½ cup boiling water

Peel and shred beets. Put raw beets in a heavy pan with vinegar, butter, mustard, shallots or green onions, tarragon, salt, and boiling water. Cover and simmer for 5 minutes, or until tender. Drain, saving liquid; add salt if necessary, pour over beets, and serve. Makes 6 to 8 servings.

Beets with Apples

Here's a new way with beets that's particularly good when you serve them with liver, meat loaf, or tongue.

Chop 1 medium-sized onion and brown lightly in ¼ cup butter. Add 4 apples, diced, and 1 bunch beets, cooked and diced. Season to taste with salt and freshly grated nutmeg, cover, and simmer until the apples are tender but not mushy. Makes 6 servings.

Brussels Sprouts with Chestnuts

This is a classic combination that can be made with the dried chestnuts found in Italian or Chinese markets. Dried chestnuts are already shelled and skinned, but it is sometimes necessary to pick out some of the skin that is lurking in the interstices after they are cooked.

Soak chestnuts overnight in warm water. Drain. Cover with water, bring to a boil, and cook until tender (about 1 hour). Dice 1 cup cooked chestnuts and brown lightly in 2 tablespoons butter; add ½ teaspoon each salt and sugar and a few drops lemon juice. Toss with 1 pound cooked fresh Brussels sprouts. Makes 4 servings.

Celery and Pecan Ring

You can serve this ring hot, its center filled with creamed mushrooms, sweetbreads, chicken, shrimp, crab, or lobster, or serve it cold, filled with chicken, lobster, shrimp, or crab salad.

1 cup fine dry bread crumbs
1½ cups ground celery
2 tablespoons ground parsley
¾ cup ground pecans
⅓ cup ground onion
⅓ cup ground green pepper (or less)
3 large eggs
3 tablespoons melted butter
1½ teaspoons salt
Pepper
1½ cups milk

Combine bread crumbs, ground celery, parsley, pecans, onion, green pepper, eggs, butter, salt, pepper, and milk. Beat together thoroughly, then pour into a well-buttered 8½-inch (5-cup) ring mold. Let stand for 30 minutes. Put into a larger pan containing hot water, and bake in a moderate oven (350°) for 1 hour. Let stand in hot water for 10 minutes before unmolding. Serve at once or chill. Makes 6 to 8 servings.

Bits of chopped ham or crisp bacon, or sautéed onions, are good mixed with peas, and so, too, are bits of red pimiento, sautéed sliced mushrooms, or lightly cooked, finely sliced celery.

Crisp Shredded Carrots

The "cut" of a vegetable makes a big difference in the way it is cooked and the way it tastes. If you shave carrots with a vegetable peeler, or shred them on a grater, they will cook tender-crisp in 2 or 3 minutes, and they'll have quite a different flavor from carrots cooked by other methods.

Cook the shredded or shaved carrots, covered, in a minimum of water for 2 or 3 minutes. Drain off any remaining water, dress with butter and minced parsley or thyme or chives, and season with salt and pepper.

Carrots Cointreau

Here's another way to make the ordinary carrot special. Carrots go well with most main dishes, but Carrots Cointreau are especially good with roast turkey or duck.

Scrape 2 bunches medium-sized carrots and slice them thin, on the diagonal. Cook, covered, in a minimum of water until tender-crisp; drain, and dress with ¼ cup each melted butter and Cointreau. Makes 6 to 8 servings.

Tiny new potatoes may be varied in many ways: Boil them unpeeled in salted water until just tender, then dress them with melted butter and any of the following: chopped chives and parsley in equal amounts; chopped parsley and mint in equal amounts; caraway seeds; grated Parmesan cheese; toasted bread crumbs; chopped walnuts; chopped dill; curry powder; coarsely ground fresh pepper; or chopped green olives.

Carrots and Caraway

Caraway seeds add wonderful flavor to carrots. This dish is easy to make and suitable for guests or family.

Cook 2 tablespoons minced onions in 2 tablespoons butter until wilted. Add 2 tablespoons flour, mix smooth, then add 1 cup beef stock or bouillon and ½ to 1 teaspoon caraway seeds. Simmer for 10 minutes, then combine with 3 cups sliced or diced cooked carrots. Heat and serve. Makes 6 servings.

Flemish Carrots

Carrots become dinner party fare when prepared in the Flemish manner.

Cut 1 pound scraped carrots in julienne strips. Put in a heavy pan with ¼ cup water and 2 tablespoons butter. Cover and cook until carrots are barely tender and the liquid has evaporated. Beat 2 egg yolks into ½ cup whipping cream, add 1 teaspoon lemon juice; add to the carrots. Heat gently, stirring, until the sauce thickens. Sprinkle with minced fresh parsley and serve at once. Makes about 4 servings.

Carrots Nivernaise

Peas and carrots are a vegetable combination with no particular charm except, perhaps, in color. But done this way, in the manner of France's Nivernaise region, they are a gastronomic delight.

Put ¼ pound butter in a saucepan with 3 pounds fresh peas, shelled; 1 dozen very small white onions or the white bulbs of green onions; the small, pale inner leaves of 2 bunches Boston or butter lettuce, cut in strips; 6 baby carrots, cut in ½-inch slices (or a dozen small round "French" carrots); ½ cup water; ½ teaspoon sugar; and ½ teaspoon salt. Cover and cook over low heat for 30 minutes, or until the vegetables are tender. In the meantime, simmer 1 cup cream until it is reduced one-half. Arrange the carrots and onions around the edge of a dish, add the cream to the peas and lettuce, and pour into the center. Makes 6 servings.

Mushrooms Béarnaise

These delicious mushrooms are named for the sauce, created in Béarn, which tops them. The sauce can be made quickly and easily in a blender. Serve Mushrooms Béarnaise as a garnish for steak or chicken—or put each mushroom on a round of toast and serve as an appetizer.

Clean 1 pound (24 to 30) medium-sized mushrooms and remove stems. Sauté lightly in 2 tablespoons butter. Remove and keep warm. Clean ¾ pound chicken livers, separate liver halves, and cut each half into two pieces. Sauté in the same pan, adding butter if necessary. Season with salt and pepper to taste, and put a piece in each mushroom cap; arrange in a baking dish.

Put in a slow oven (275° to 300°) while making sauce: In blender, combine 3 egg yolks, 1½ tablespoons tarragon vinegar, and 3 tablespoons chopped parsley. Melt ¾ cup butter and heat until it bubbles—don't brown. Add 1 tablespoon hot water to egg yolks and vinegar; turn blender on high speed and immediately pour in the hot butter in a steady stream. Add ½ teaspoon salt, a dash of cayenne, and 1 teaspoon prepared mustard; whirl until well blended—about 30 seconds. (Sauce may be reheated in top of a double boiler over hot but not boiling water; stir until smooth and warm.) Top each mushroom with a dab of the sauce, and serve hot.

Chestnut Purée

This is a delicious and different dish to serve with roast meats. It is particularly good with venison.

Remove outer shells and inner skins from the desired number of chestnuts, first making a slit in their shells and boiling them for 10 minutes. (Keep them in hot water and shell one at a time.) Cover peeled chestnuts with boiling salted water or chicken stock, and simmer until tender, from 20 to 30 minutes—a little overcooking will not matter.

When chestnuts are tender, force them through a ricer or mash them well. For each 2 cups of mashed chestnuts (the usual yield from 1 pound of chestnuts), add ¼ cup butter or margarine and enough cream (about ½ cup) to make them the consistency of soft mashed potatoes. Beat until fluffy, season with salt to taste, and reheat before serving.

Okra, also called "gumbo" or "gombo," gave its name to the famous Louisiana stew, which was originally made with it. Today gumbos do not necessarily contain okra; filé powder, the dried leaves of the sassafras, may be used in its place. Both have the same thickening qualities.

Eggplant Casserole

Here's a flavorful eggplant casserole that can be made in advance and baked just before serving.

Peel and cube 1 large eggplant; sauté in ¼ cup each olive oil and butter until browned. Rub a 2-quart earthenware casserole thoroughly with a crushed clove of garlic, and add the eggplant. Sauté 1 cup minced onion in the pan in which the eggplant was cooked, adding a little more shortening if necessary. Add to the casserole, along with 3 large peeled and diced tomatoes. Season with ½ teaspoon basil, 1½ teaspoons salt, and a little pepper. Mix gently and top with ½ cup fine dry bread crumbs mixed with 1 tablespoon melted butter or oil (or top with ½ cup shredded Cheddar cheese). Bake in a moderately hot oven (375°) for 30 minutes, or until brown. Makes 6 servings.

Braised Endive

Belgium endive, though expensive, is so compact that a little goes a long way. A stalk for each serving is adequate. It's a refreshing accompaniment to a richly sauced meat dish.

Wash endive, and trim any discolored part from the root end; split the stalks in two. Put endive in a skillet with 1 teaspoon melted butter and 1 teaspoon lemon juice for each stalk. Sprinkle with salt and pepper, and add enough water or stock to cover the bottom of the pan ¼ inch deep. Cover and cook for 15 minutes. Serve as is, or with a thin cream sauce.

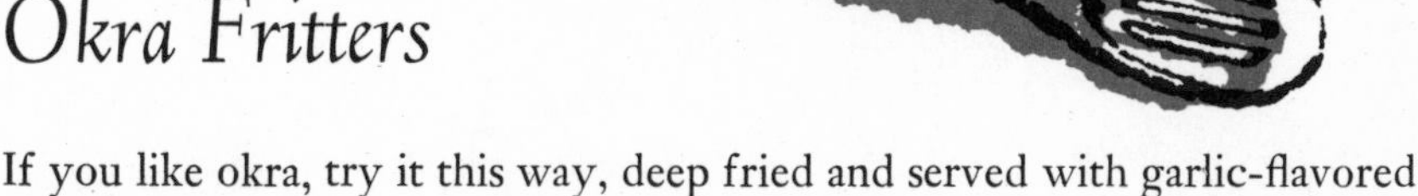

Okra Fritters

If you like okra, try it this way, deep fried and served with garlic-flavored melted butter. Use young okra, with tender pods.

Make a batter with 1 cup flour, ½ teaspoon salt, 1 teaspoon baking powder, 2 tablespoons olive oil, ¾ cup milk, and 1 well-beaten egg. Wash and dry 1 pound small okra pods, remove stems, and split in halves. Dust lightly with seasoned flour (½ cup flour, ½ teaspoon salt, and a little pepper), then dip in the fritter batter. Fry one in deep fat at 370° to test batter consistency; it should be thick enough to cling, thin enough to form only a light, crisp crust when fried. Correct batter by adding either flour or water, as necessary. Serve with melted butter, seasoned with 1 clove crushed garlic. Makes 4 servings.

Onions au Gratin

In this case, the "gratin" means, as it so often does in France, browned crumbs of bread rather than of cheese. This is good with charcoal-broiled meats or fish.

Peel and cook 4 pounds onions until tender. Drain and chop; mix with 5 chopped hard-cooked eggs, 2 cups Béchamel sauce (page 152), and salt, pepper, and tarragon to taste. Pour into an 8-inch-square baking dish, sprinkle with 1 cup dried bread crumbs which have been mixed with 3 tablespoons melted butter. Bake in a moderately hot oven (375°) until browned. Makes 8 to 10 servings.

French-fried Green Pepper Rings

We all know how good French-fried onions are, but not too many have tried French-fried green pepper rings. Serve them with roast lamb, lamb chops, or meat loaf.

Slice the peppers crosswise in ½-inch rings. Remove seeds and discard end pieces. Dip the rings in milk and then in seasoned flour (1 teaspoon salt and ¼ teaspoon pepper to 1 cup flour). Fry in hot, deep fat (360°) until brown, about 1 minute. Drain on paper towels, and sprinkle with salt.

Marinated Green Peppers

Try these at your next patio party. They are just right with grilled meats. Allow 1 large green pepper for every 2 persons to be served.

To give the green peppers the full benefit of the marinade, it is necessary to skin them. Char them thoroughly over a flame, wrap in several layers of paper and then in a towel, and cool. Rub off outer skin. Cut peppers in halves, discard stems and seeds, and slice lengthwise. For every 3 peppers, combine ⅓ cup olive oil, 2 tablespoons mild wine vinegar, ½ teaspoon salt, and a little freshly ground pepper. Pour over peppers and let stand for at least 1 hour before serving. Do not chill.

Potatoes with Capers

Considering the fact that each caper is the tiny bud of a plant and has to be hand picked, it is surprising that this pickled condiment is so inexpensive. It's well worth keeping on hand for the interesting sharp flavor it can add to many dishes—boiled potatoes, for instance.

For 6 medium-sized potatoes, melt ¼ cup butter and add 1 tablespoon chopped capers. Mix with the hot potatoes before serving.

Patio Potatoes

Chilies and Cheddar cheese make this savory potato casserole an especially satisfying accompaniment to charcoal-grilled meats.

2½ pounds potatoes
3 cups medium cream sauce
2 cups shredded mild Cheddar cheese
1 can (4 oz.) peeled green chilies, rinsed and cut in pieces
2 teaspoons salt
2 puréed cloves garlic
Buttered crumbs

Cook potatoes; peel, slice (or cube), and put into a 1½-quart baking dish. Combine cream sauce, cheese, chilies, salt, and garlic. Cook, stirring, until cheese is melted; pour cheese mixture over potatoes. Sprinkle top with buttered crumbs and bake in a moderate oven (350°) until hot and brown. Makes 6 to 8 servings.

Pink Potatoes

Don't let the name fool you. These are not for a ladies' luncheon! They're men's fare, good with roast pork or with mutton chops.

Cook 1 chopped onion until wilted in 2 tablespoons butter. Force through a sieve (or whirl in a blender), and add 1 cup sour cream and at least 2 tablespoons paprika. Boil 2 pounds potatoes, then mash well, using this mixture instead of the usual butter and milk. Add salt to taste; heat. Makes about 6 servings.

New Potatoes with Lemon

Next time you cook small new potatoes, try dressing them with a mixture of 6 tablespoons melted butter, 1 teaspoon grated lemon peel, and 1 tablespoon each minced chives and lemon juice. These are particularly good with fish or lamb chops.

Hungarian Potato Pie

Layers of potatoes and egg slices make up this hearty side dish casserole. Try it when steak or chicken is the *pièce de résistance.*

Boil 1 pound potatoes until just tender; drain and peel, then cut in thin slices. Hard cook 3 eggs and slice. Generously butter bottom and sides of a shallow baking dish (about 1½-quart size), then sprinkle with crumbs, tipping so that the crumbs adhere to the sides as well as the bottom. Arrange a layer of potatoes in the bottom, sprinkle with salt and pepper, and cover with egg slices. Sprinkle with ¼ cup chopped, cooked ham. Make another layer with the remaining potatoes, eggs, and another ¼ cup ham. Beat 1 egg yolk and mix with 1 cup sour cream; pour over all. Sprinkle with about ¼ cup fine dry bread crumbs that have been mixed with about 2 tablespoons melted butter. Bake in a moderate oven (350°) for 20 to 25 minutes. Makes 6 servings.

Onion Mashed Potatoes

This is so simple that it can hardly be called a recipe, but it's a delicious way to vary mashed potatoes. The potatoes can be browned in a casserole, if you wish.

Allow 1 large onion for every 2 pounds potatoes. Dice the onion and lightly brown it in ¼ cup butter. Mash potatoes as usual, but omit butter, adding the onion mixture instead.

Spinach with Raisins

This unusual recipe is from Rome. If you sauté the onion in olive oil instead of butter, you'll add to the Italian flavor.

Cook 1 medium-sized onion, chopped, in 2 tablespoons butter or olive oil until wilted. Plump 2 tablespoons seedless raisins (pour boiling water over them to cover, let stand for 15 minutes, and drain). Meanwhile, in another pan, cook 2 pounds spinach in the water that clings to its leaves. When wilted and bright green, drain and chop coarsely. Mix with the onions (including butter or oil in which they were cooked), the raisins, and 2 tablespoons pine nuts. Heat; season to taste with salt, freshly grated nutmeg, and, if you wish, additional butter. Makes 4 to 6 servings.

Spinach with Eggs

Spinach is a base for poached eggs in this dish, which can be a luncheon or supper entrée.

Cook 2 pounds spinach until tender, but still green. Drain, chop, and mix with 1 cup medium cream sauce. Season to taste and keep hot. Cook 2 tablespoons minced onion and ¼ pound mushrooms, chopped, in 1 tablespoon butter until tender. Add ½ clove garlic, puréed, and salt to taste. Toast 6 large rounds of bread and poach 6 eggs. To serve, spread hot spinach on a platter, top with the toast rounds which have been spread with the mushroom mixture, and put a poached egg on each round. Makes 6 servings.

Stuffed Zucchini

Stuffed zucchini, as it is served in Italy, makes an economical and delightful main course for a family dinner. Serve it with spaghetti, dressed simply with half butter and half olive oil.

- 12 zucchini, 5 or 6 inches long
- 1 pound ground beef
- 1 egg
- 1 clove garlic, mashed with 1½ teaspoons salt
- ½ teaspoon crumbled dried oregano
- 2 slices bread
- 3 tablespoons olive oil or shortening
- 1 cup tomato sauce
- 1 cup beef gravy
- ½ cup grated Romano or Parmesan cheese

Using an apple corer, carefully remove centers of zucchini, leaving a hollow tube. Stuff with a mixture of the beef, egg, garlic, salt, oregano, and the 2 slices of bread which have been soaked in water and squeezed dry and crumbled. Sauté squash in olive oil until lightly browned. Arrange in a baking dish; combine tomato sauce and beef gravy and pour over squash. Sprinkle with the grated cheese, and bake for 20 minutes in a moderate oven (350°), or until the cheese is nicely browned. Makes 6 servings.

Acorn Squash with Filberts

Brown sugar and orange flavors are wonderful with acorn squash, and the filberts add a pleasing texture contrast.

Select 6 uniform-sized acorn squash, cut in halves, and scrape out seeds. Combine ½ cup brown sugar, firmly packed, ½ cup butter, 1 teaspoon salt, 1 teaspoon cinnamon, 2 tablespoons grated orange peel, the juice of 2 oranges, 1 cup coarsely chopped filberts. Pour ½ inch of water in a large baking pan, add the squash, cut side up, divide mixture among the cavities, and cover with foil. Bake in a moderately hot oven (375°) for 40 minutes; uncover, spread sauce around inside of squash, and continue baking for 40 minutes, or until brown and tender. Makes 12 servings.

Green Tomatoes

Firmer and more sharply flavored than ripe tomatoes, green tomatoes are delicious when sliced, floured, and fried in bacon fat. They are also good baked this way:

Slice 8 tomatoes and arrange in layers in a baking dish, sprinkling each layer with a little of this mixture: Combine 1½ teaspoons salt, ½ teaspoon pepper, 2 tablespoons chives or 1 teaspoon mixed herbs, and ¾ cup coarse toasted bread crumbs. Dot each layer liberally with butter. Top tomatoes with about ¼ cup grated Parmesan cheese, and bake in a moderate oven (350°) for 1 hour. Makes 6 to 8 servings.

Stewed Tomatoes with Cheese

Canned tomatoes acquire real distinction when combined with crisp croûtons, melting cheese cubes, and succulent bits of green pepper.

Cook a large can (1 lb. 14 oz.) tomatoes until about ⅓ of the liquid has evaporated. Season to taste with salt and pepper, and have ready ½ cup each diced jack cheese and crisp croûtons, and 2 tablespoons diced green pepper. Just before serving, reheat the tomatoes, stir in the other ingredients, and serve.

Grains & Pastas

The recipes in this chapter give but an inkling of the various ways in which rice, wheat, corn, and other grains, can be used by the knowledgeable or imaginative cook. Then there are the pastas—noodles, spaghetti, macaroni, fettucine—for which there are enough possible uses to keep a creative cook happy for days on end. Add to these polenta, cous-cous, risotto, and other famous international dishes made with grains and pastes of one kind or another, and you have enough recipes to fill several volumes.

Grains and pastas have two main places in the American diet—as an accompaniment to a meat or poultry entrée, or as a main dish, usually combined with fish, meat, shellfish, and/or cheese in a casserole. They are particularly popular as buffet dishes or to serve with barbecue meals, and they are a boon to the cook who must keep Lenten meals from becoming tiresome.

We have included here a varied selection of outstanding recipes using grains and pastas. The cook who enjoys culinary adventures will almost certainly create many more delicious and fascinating ones.

Kitchree

Sometimes spelled *kitchri*, this is the forerunner of kedgeree, a mixture of rice and fish quite popular in England as a breakfast dish. Kitchree is Indian, a mixture of rice and *dhal*, or lentils, rice, and spices; it is delicious served in place of rice with a curry.

Wash 1 cup of lentils and parboil for 10 minutes. Slice 2 large onions and cook until lightly browned in ½ cup (¼ pound) butter, sprinkling with 2 teaspoons salt toward the end of the cooking. Remove onions from butter with a slotted spoon and keep warm. To the same pan, add 1½ cups uncooked rice, the drained lentils, and 2 tablespoons finely sliced fresh ginger root. Cook over low heat until the butter is absorbed (about 5 minutes).

Make a cheesecloth bag containing a 2-inch stick cinnamon, 3 whole cloves, 6 whole peppers, 1 bay leaf, and 6 whole cardamoms. Add to rice and lentils; barely cover with boiling water. Simmer, covered, until the water is absorbed and the rice and lentils are tender (about 20 minutes). You may have to add more water. Stir the mixture occasionally with a long-tined fork. When done, uncover and keep warm in a very low oven (250°). Arrange on a hot dish, strew the cooked onions over the top, and garnish with 2 sliced hard-cooked eggs. Makes 8 servings.

Next time you have wild ducks, serve them with brown rice that has been mixed with toasted sesame seed, or buttered toast crumbs, or chopped nuts of any kind.

Breakfast Rice Ring

For a festive Sunday brunch, serve this rice ring filled with scrambled eggs and garnished with crisp bacon and sautéed chicken livers.

Melt 3 tablespoons butter or margarine in a heavy pan, add 1½ cups rice, and cook, stirring, for about 10 minutes, or until the rice begins to color. Add 3 cups well-seasoned chicken stock, cover, and cook until the rice is tender. If still moist, uncover and allow to dry in a very slow oven (275°). Add salt if needed, and a little melted butter if you wish. Pack into a lightly buttered 6-cup ring mold, then unmold on a hot plate. Fill and garnish as suggested above. Makes 6 servings.

Risotto

In Italy a typical northern meal is as different from a southern one as is a New Mexico meal from one cooked in Maine. For instance, there are parts of Italy where macaroni and other *pastas* are practically unknown, and where rice plays an important role. In Milan, risotto is a favorite dish. It goes well with charcoal-broiled or roasted meat, and it's a good choice for a buffet. If you add bits of ham, chicken livers, and/or mushrooms, risotto can be a main dish.

½ cup chopped onion
½ cup butter
1½ cups uncooked rice
6 cups well-seasoned chicken stock (made with chicken bouillon cubes, or from backs and necks of chickens)
¼ teaspoon powdered saffron
Salt, if necessary
1 cup grated Parmesan cheese

Brown onion in ¼ cup of the butter, then stir in rice. Stir and cook until the rice has a translucent look and the butter is absorbed. Dissolve saffron in 1 tablespoon of the chicken stock and add it to the rice. Then pour in half the stock, cover, and cook over low heat. When the liquid is absorbed, add remainder of the stock and continue cooking until the rice is tender and not too dry. Add the remaining ¼ cup of butter and salt if necessary, and just before serving, stir in the cheese. Makes 6 servings.

Rice and Pine Nuts

Pine nuts are expensive, but just a few of them lift rice out of the realm of the ordinary. Next time you have a wild rice appetite and a plain rice pocketbook, compromise just a little and see what pine nuts will do.

Cook brown rice until tender; drain and mix each cupful with 1 tablespoon melted butter, salt and pepper to taste, and 2 tablespoons shelled pine nuts. Mix well and serve with any game or poultry.

Shrimp Rice with Asparagus

Asparagus, shrimp, rice, and tomatoes combine to make a dish that will star at a buffet. This buffet spectacular serves 12, and most of it can be prepared the day before the party. (In fact, several items require overnight refrigeration or marinating.)

1 pound rice
2 pounds fresh shrimp
½ cup each olive oil and salad oil
⅓ cup wine vinegar
1½ teaspoons salt
Freshly ground pepper
½ clove garlic, puréed
3 pounds asparagus
12 medium-small tomatoes
Salt
2 hard-cooked egg yolks, sieved

Cook rice until tender, rinse under cold water, cover, and refrigerate overnight. Cook shrimp; shell, clean, and, if large, cut into pieces. Make French dressing with the olive oil, salad oil, wine vinegar, salt, pepper, and garlic. Pour all but ½ cup of this over the shrimp and marinate in the refrigerator overnight.

Clean asparagus and cut off the tender tips (about 4 inches). (Use remaining asparagus for a soup or, sliced, for a vegetable another time.) Cook tips in salted water until *just* tender, about 7 or 8 minutes. Drain at once and cover with ¼ cup of the French dressing; cover and marinate overnight.

On the morning of the party, peel tomatoes, scoop out centers, sprinkle with salt, turn upside-down to drain, and put in the refrigerator. Before serving time, combine shrimp and rice; taste and add seasoning if needed. Arrange in the center of a large platter. Stand 3 or 4 asparagus tips in each tomato and arrange around the rice. Put remaining asparagus on top of the rice, and garnish with the sieved egg yolks. Divide remaining French dressing among the tomatoes. Makes 12 servings.

Korean Rice and Bean Sprouts

Rice is invariably an important part of a Korean meal, and Korean cooks vary it with such additions as peas, cubes of white or sweet potato, sliced mushrooms, or, as in this recipe, bean sprouts. The sesame seed is typical of Korean cookery.

- 3 tablespoons sesame seed
- 2 green onions, minced
- 1 clove garlic, minced or mashed
- 1 tablespoon sesame oil (or other bland oil)
- 1 ½ cups bean sprouts
- 2 cups cooked rice
- 2 tablespoons soy sauce

Toast sesame seed in a heavy frying pan, stirring, until they brown and puff slightly. Crush in a mortar with a pestle (or in a bowl with a wooden spoon). Combine with onion and garlic and cook in the oil for 3 minutes. Add the bean sprouts and heat. (It may be necessary to add a few drops of water or stock to keep ingredients from sticking.) Combine with the hot rice and soy sauce, and mix well. Makes 6 servings.

Cracked Wheat Casserole

A casserole that goes well with charcoal-broiled or roasted meat is a useful addition to any cook's repertoire. This one uses quick-cooking cracked wheat; or, if you enjoy lusty wheat flavor, try it with kasha or buckwheat grits.

Brown 2 cups quick-cooking cracked wheat (or kasha or buckwheat grits) in a heavy, dry skillet, stirring until it gives off a fragrance of toasting nuts. Mince 1 large onion and cook in 3 tablespoons butter until wilted. Put in a 2 or 3-quart casserole with the wheat and 4 cups beef stock. Add 1 pound sliced mushrooms, cover, and bake in a moderate oven (350°) for about 45 minutes. Correct seasoning with salt and pepper. Serve hot with cold sour cream. Makes 10 or 12 servings.

Cous-cous

This dish, common in Algeria and Morocco, has many different versions.

You will need a steamer or kettle large enough to contain the broth, meats, and vegetables (these total about 4 quarts), with space above it to steam the grain, which shouldn't touch the liquid (suspend the grain in a colander, strainer, or steamer). A few specialty food stores sell a special wheat product called cous-cous (or sometimes *faufel*), in either the uncooked form or an instant form (called tout prêt). Farina, though finer than cous-cous, can be used quite satisfactorily, and so can cracked wheat.

4 large onions, cut into chunks
¼ cup butter
1½ pounds boneless lamb shoulder, cut into 6 pieces
1 broiler-fryer, cut into pieces (breasts should be quartered)
2 teaspoons salt
¼ teaspoon pepper
Liquid hot-pepper seasoning or cayenne
¼ teaspoon powdered ginger
About 4 cups water
2 turnips, peeled and cut into chunks
4 carrots, peeled and cut into chunks
2 zucchinis and/or 2 artichoke bottoms, cut into pieces (optional)
1 cup uncooked or instant (tout prêt) cous-cous, or farina, or cracked wheat
2 tablespoons butter
Additional salt to taste

Brown onions lightly in the ¼ cup butter. Put in the bottom of the steamer. In the pan in which the onions cooked, brown the lamb and the chicken, adding more butter if needed. (Set aside the pan without washing it—you'll use it once again.) Add lamb to onions along with the salt, pepper, a dash of liquid hot-pepper seasoning or cayenne, and the ginger. Cover with water and simmer for 30 to 40 minutes; add the chicken, turnips, carrots, and the zucchini or artichoke bottoms, if used.

If you use uncooked cous-cous or farina or cracked wheat, soak in water for about 10 minutes, drain, and put in the top of the steamer, laying several thicknesses of cheesecloth over the holes of the steamer, if necessary. Cover, wrap a wet strip of cloth around lid of steamer, and steam for 45 or 50 minutes, or until chicken is tender. If you use instant cous-cous, rinse with water and add for the last 15 minutes of cooking.

When meat is done, melt the 2 tablespoons butter in the pan in which the onions and meat were browned; mix with cous-cous, adding salt to taste, if needed. To serve, heap cous-cous in center of a large platter; surround with meat and vegetables, and serve broth, with salt added if necessary, to be drunk with the cous-cous. Makes 6 generous servings.

Homemade Noodles

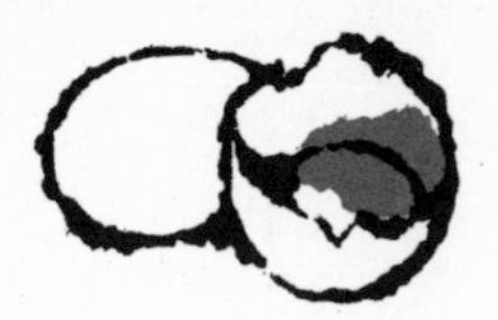

Once you've tried homemade egg noodles, you'll never be completely satisfied with any other kind. They're really not very difficult to make. Cooks interested in gadgets might like to invest in a pasta machine, sold in Italian import stores. With one of these machines, noodles are quite easy to make. You mix the ingredients as below, then roll in the machine. The thin sheets of noodle dough are then put through another set of rollers to cut them thick or thin, depending on which set of cutters you use.

Sift 2 cups flour and ¾ teaspoon salt onto a pastry board or table top. Beat 2 large eggs slightly, and pour into a hole or well made in the center of the flour. Knead, gradually working in all of the egg, until you have a smooth but soft dough. To get the right consistency, it may be necessary to add 1 to 2 tablespoons of water. Knead well, then divide into 2 or 3 parts, and roll paper thin. Let rest on the board for about 10 minutes, then roll like a jelly roll and slice thinly for narrow noodles, thicker for wide ones. Let dry, turning occasionally so they won't stick. Cook in salted water in the usual manner.

At the famous Alfredo alla Scrofa restaurant in Rome, Alfredo himself mixes the fettucine. He uses a gold fork and spoon that was presented to him many years ago by Mary Pickford and Douglas Fairbanks.

Noodles with Mushrooms

This is very simple, good, and different.

Cook 1 package (8 oz.) egg noodles until tender; drain and rinse in hot water. Put in a rather shallow buttered baking dish. Clean and chop 1 pound mushrooms, stems and all. Sauté in 3 tablespoons butter until almost dry. Add ½ cup toast crumbs, mix well, season with salt and pepper, and add 1 tablespoon melted butter. Cover noodles with the hot mushroom mixture; sprinkle with parsley, and serve or keep warm in the oven until serving time. Makes about 6 servings.

Fettucine alla Romana

As travelers to Italy know, the fettucine served in Rome is par excellence. One reason is that the noodles are fresh; another, that the Parmesan cheese is freshly grated. Still another secret is the addition of plenty of butter and cream.

Make 1 recipe fresh egg noodles (page 61), cutting the rolled-out noodle dough into strips ½ inch wide. Boil until tender in plenty of salted water to which you've added 1 tablespoon of olive oil. Don't overcook; 4 or 5 minutes should be ample. Drain the noodles and dress at once with ¼ cup butter cut into slices; ½ cup heavy cream, slightly whipped; and ¾ cup of freshly grated Parmesan cheese. Mix by lifting the noodles high in the air with a fork and spoon again and again until every strand is covered. Serve immediately. Makes 4 generous servings.

Parsley and Bacon Fettucine

If you're fond of bacon, you've probably discovered that bacon fat is worth saving to cook with. Here's a simple fettucine dish that makes the most of the flavor rapport between pasta, bacon, and cheese. Serve it as a main course with broiled tomatoes or fried green peppers.

Dice 8 slices bacon and fry until crisp. Drain on paper towels, but save fat (keep hot). Purée 1 small clove garlic and add it and 1 cup minced parsley to ½ of the bacon fat. Cook 1 pound fettucine until just tender, drain thoroughly and mix with the bacon and parsley mixture. Mix gently but well, working quickly so it won't cool. Add more hot bacon fat if the pasta is not completely dressed. Serve at once with freshly grated Parmesan cheese. Makes 8 servings.

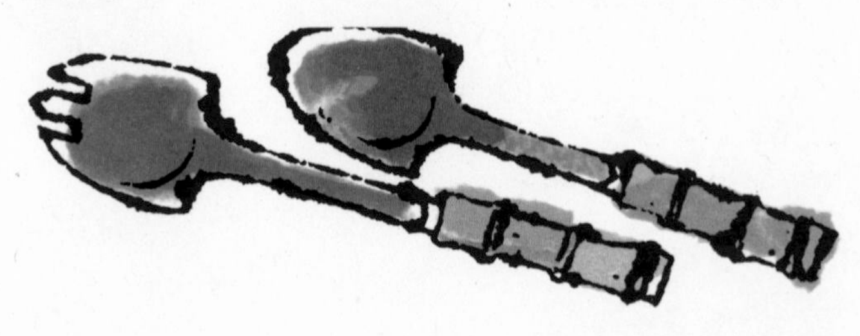

Pasticcio di Polenta

Polenta pie makes an excellent casserole for a buffet, to serve with baked ham, roast capon, or turkey. Make polenta the day before serving.

2 quarts boiling water
1 tablespoon salt
2 cups corn meal (either white or yellow)
¼ cup butter
1 cup fine dry bread crumbs
1 pound fresh mushrooms, sliced
3 tablespoons butter
Salt
6 tablespoons grated Parmesan cheese
½ cup plus 1 tablespoon light cream
Butter
Chopped parsley

Add salt to boiling water, and sprinkle in corn meal. Cook, stirring, until thick—the standard test in Italy is to cook until a wooden spoon will stand upright in the mush. (It can be cooked over hot water, in which case allow 1½ hours.) When polenta is sufficiently thick, pour it into a 3½ or 4-quart round casserole (one in which the finished dish may be served). Chill thoroughly.

When ready to complete the "pie," turn polenta out of the casserole and slice into four even layers. (The easiest way to do this is with a piece of string.) Butter the casserole thickly with the ¼ cup butter, and sprinkle with ⅓ cup of the bread crumbs. Put the top slice of polenta in the bottom of the casserole (the slice that was on the bottom of the casserole originally). Spread ⅓ of the sliced mushrooms on this layer, dot with 1 tablespoon of the butter, sprinkle with salt and 2 tablespoons of the cheese, and pour 3 tablespoons of the cream evenly over the top. Add the next layer of polenta and repeat, adding another ⅓ cup of the mushrooms and the same amounts of butter, salt, cheese, and cream. Repeat again. Dot the top layer generously with butter; cover, and bake in a moderate oven (350°) for 1½ hours. Before serving, sprinkle chopped parsley on top, if you wish. Serve piping hot. Makes 12 to 15 servings.

Malfatti

Malfatti means "badly made" in Italian, and the dish was apparently discovered by some cook who was trying to make ravioli, but botched the job. Botched or not, it's a delicious dish, and far easier to make than most fresh pastas. Serve it, with melted butter and freshly grated cheese, as an accompaniment for meat, either oven-cooked or charcoal-broiled; or top it with the rich sauce and serve it as the main dish for a family meal or party buffet. Malfatti freezes well. You can freeze the cylinders, then thaw and dust with flour again before poaching; or you can freeze the assembled dish after you have poached the malfatti and covered them with the sauce, then reheat, covered, in a very hot oven. This recipe makes about 40 malfatti, or enough for 10 to 16 people.

2 cups lightly-cooked and well-drained chopped spinach (about 1¼ pounds fresh spinach, or two 10-ounce packages frozen chopped spinach)
1 pound ricotta cheese
¼ of a whole nutmeg, grated, or ½ teaspoon ground nutmeg
½ cup minced green onions, including tender part of tops
1 tablespoon minced fresh basil, or 2 teaspoons dried basil
2½ cups soft bread crumbs
½ cup minced fresh parsley
¼ cup freshly grated Romano cheese
1 large clove garlic, pressed
1½ teaspoons salt
3 eggs
Flour

Mix together all ingredients except flour. Form into cylinders about 3 inches long and ¾ inch in diameter. Roll in flour and arrange on waxed paper on a cooky sheet, taking care that cylinders do not touch each other. Let stand in the refrigerator for 12 to 24 hours. Poach, a few at a time, in simmering salted water. Cook for 6 to 8 minutes, or until malfatti come to the top of the water. Lift out with a slotted spoon; drain well, and arrange on a serving dish, keeping warm until all the malfatti are cooked. Serve with melted butter and freshly grated cheese, or with the following sauce.

Sauce: Soak 6 dried Italian mushrooms in ½ cup hot water for 2 or 3 hours. Cut into small dice, saving the liquid. Cook 1 large finely minced clove garlic and ½ cup chopped onion in 3 tablespoons olive oil and 1 tablespoon butter until the onion is soft. Add the mushrooms and mushroom water, a quarter of a nutmeg, grated, ½ teaspoon fennel seed crushed in a mortar, a dash of liquid hot-pepper seasoning, 1 teaspoon oregano, 2 cans (8 oz. each) tomato sauce, 1 can (10½ oz.) consommé or beef bouillon, 1 teaspoon salt, ½ cup minced green pepper, and ¼ cup minced parsley. Simmer for 20 minutes, correct seasoning, and pour over malfatti.

Spaghetti Furiosa

Here's a spaghetti dish that is out of the ordinary.

Combine 2 cans (8 oz. each) tomato sauce, ½ cup minced onion, 1 pressed clove of garlic, 2 tablespoons olive oil, and 1 teaspoon basil, and simmer until thickened. Add salt and pepper to taste. Combine with 2 cans (7 oz. each) flaked tuna, 1 can (4 oz.) minced ripe olives, ¼ cup minced green olives, 2 tablespoons capers, and 4 anchovies cut into pieces. Simmer while boiling 12 ounces of spaghetti *al dente*. Drain spaghetti, put on a platter, and pour the sauce over all. Makes 6 servings.

Spaghetti alla Vongole

This is spaghetti with a clam sauce.

Heat ⅓ cup olive oil with 1 crushed clove of garlic. Add 1 small chopped onion and sauté until wilted. Add juice from 2 cans (7 oz. each) minced clams and ⅓ cup tomato paste; simmer for 20 minutes. Add clams, and cook for 1 minute; then stir in ⅓ cup minced parsley. Meanwhile, cook 1 pound spaghetti *al dente*; drain, and mix in the clam sauce. Pass freshly grated Parmesan cheese. Makes 6 to 8 servings.

Cannoli and cannelloni are often confused; their names are similar—in fact, they come from the same word, which means hollow tube, pipe, or reed. There is a large hollow Italian macaroni called "cannelloni," but the dish by that name, as it is served in Italy, is most often either squares of noodle paste or thin pancakes, filled with a savory meat filling and masked with a tomato sauce or a creamy cheese sauce that is browned under the broiler. Cannoli, on the other hand, is a Sicilian dessert: tubes of flaky pastry filled with a delectable Ricotta cheese and chocolate mixture.

Macaroni al Latte

This is more or less the same thing as "macaroni and cheese" which used to be very popular at the turn of the century.

Cook 12 ounces macaroni in salted water until just tender, or *al dente*. Drain. Cook together ¼ cup butter and 2 tablespoons flour until they turn golden. Then gradually stir in 3 cups milk. Simmer, stirring, for 10 minutes, then add 1 ounce (⅓ cup) grated Parmesan cheese and the drained macaroni. Mix well and simmer for 5 minutes, then add 3 tablespoons more butter and 1½ ounces (½ cup) more grated cheese.

Put in a 3-quart baking dish, cover with about ½ cup buttered, soft bread crumbs, and put in a hot oven (400°) for about 20 minutes or until browned. Makes about 12 servings.

Macaroni with Ricotta Cheese

This is good with charcoal-broiled meats.

Cook 1 pound macaroni *al dente*. Drain and mix with ¼ cup melted butter or margarine. Blend 1 pound Ricotta cheese with ½ cup milk and ½ teaspoon salt. Mix with the macaroni, cover, and cook very slowly for 5 minutes. Serve from a heated bowl, and sprinkle with ¼ cup grated Parmesan cheese. Makes 6 to 8 servings.

Hominy and Chili Casserole

Here's a robust casserole that goes especially well with ham. But it's good with broiled chicken, too, and with spareribs.

Drain 2 cans (1 lb. each) whole white hominy; mix carefully with 2 tablespoons grated onion, 1 cup cream sauce, 1 cup coarsely shredded jack cheese, 4 canned peeled green chilies, rinsed of their seeds and cut into small pieces, and salt to taste. Put into a 1½-quart casserole, sprinkle the top with about ¼ cup dry bread crumbs, dot with 2 tablespoons butter, and bake in a moderate oven (350°) for about 30 minutes, or until hot. Set under the broiler briefly, if necessary, to brown top. Makes 6 to 8 servings.

Eggs & Cheese

Chefs of eminence treat the egg with as much respect as they accord to the most expensive cut of meat. A perfect poached, scrambled, or mollet egg is a work of art, and to make a flawless omelette takes many days of practice—but what a sense of accomplishment once you've mastered it! Eggs take well to saucing, too, and classic recipes for egg dishes number into the hundreds.

To cook without eggs would be difficult indeed, and the results dreary, for eggs perform many culinary functions. They bind, leaven, enrich, thicken, garnish, and they play the leading role in innumerable famous dishes. Here you'll find some classic recipes for eggs, and some from other lands to prove that they are a world-wide delicacy.

Cheese, too, is a versatile and invaluable cooking ingredient. It is used, in one form or another, in almost every part of the world. Sometimes it plays a major role; but the skilled cook has other, and subtler uses for it, too. It is sprinkled atop a creamy dish to gratinée it, added to a sauce to accent an otherwise bland dish, and used to complement, to refine, or to improve the flavor of a multitude of dishes, from soup to dessert.

Poached Deviled Eggs

These are deviled eggs that are not hard-cooked. They make a very good luncheon dish.

Make 1 cup Béchamel sauce (page 152) or medium cream sauce, and to it add ¼ cup chopped chutney. Spread 4 slices of toast with butter that has been creamed with a little curry powder (1 teaspoon to ¼ cup), top each with a nicely poached egg, and pour the sauce over all. Makes 4 servings.

If you don't have an egg-poaching pan, you can keep poached eggs tidy by cooking them in muffin rings or flat cans that have had both top and bottom removed with an edge-turning can opener. Simply put the lightly greased rings in the skillet of salted water and drop an egg in each.

Poached Eggs Provencal

Ripe tomatoes are responsible for the fresh flavor of Poached Eggs Provençal, a fine breakfast or luncheon dish.

- 4 large ripe tomatoes
- 2 tablespoons each butter and olive oil
- 1 small clove garlic, puréed
- 1 tablespoon minced parsley
- ½ teaspoon salt
- Pepper
- 4 poached eggs
- Grated Parmesan cheese

Peel tomatoes, cut them in halves crosswise, and gently squeeze out the seeds. Cut in dice and put in a flame-proof shallow baking dish with the butter and olive oil. Cook over direct heat for 3 or 4 minutes; add garlic, parsley, salt, and a dash of pepper. Cook for 1 minute; top with poached eggs. Sprinkle eggs (not the sauce) with grated Parmesan cheese; set under broiler until cheese browns. Makes 4 servings.

Pipérade

The Basques have some dishes that are their very own. One is Pipérade, an egg dish that is a sort of cross between scrambled eggs and an omelette. Methods of preparation vary, but this is the general idea.

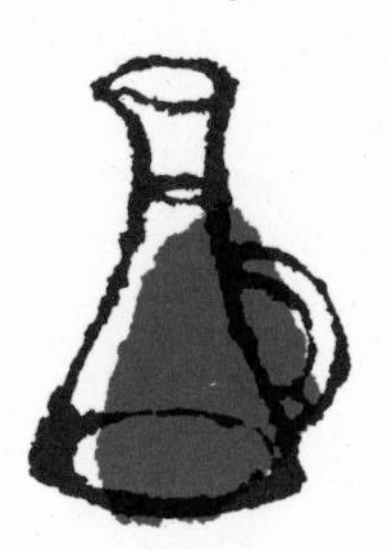

- 1 small green pepper, chopped
- 1 onion, chopped
- 1 tomato, peeled, seeded, and chopped
- 3 tablespoons olive oil
- 1 small sweet red pepper, chopped or 1 canned pimiento, chopped
- 2 tablespoons chopped ham
- 1 tablespoon butter or margarine
- 4 eggs, slightly beaten and seasoned with salt and pepper to taste

Sauté green pepper, onion, and tomato in oil. Add red pepper or pimiento, and ham; cook slowly for 15 minutes, then add butter and eggs. Stir enough to mix with the vegetables, then cook slowly until eggs set. Turn out of the pan onto a platter and serve at once. Makes 3 or 4 servings.

Eggs Surprise

This dish is made from leftovers, plus a few eggs.

Spread mashed potatoes about 1½ inches deep in a shallow buttered baking dish. Using the bottom of a glass or cup, make six indentations in the potatoes. Half fill each well with leftovers—minced meat, poultry, or fish, mixed with gravy or sour cream, and nicely seasoned, or leftover cooked vegetables. Drop an egg in each depression. Sprinkle the whole with melted butter and, if you wish, with shredded cheese. Heat in a moderate oven (350°) for 15 minutes, or until the eggs are just set and the potatoes hot and slightly browned; serve with or without tomato sauce. Makes 6 servings.

Cheese and Ripe Olive Soufflé

This cheese-flavored soufflé is flavored with minced ripe olives. For a Mexican touch, you can add 2 or 3 tablespoons of minced peeled green chilies (the canned kind) along with the olives.

2 tablespoons butter
2 tablespoons flour
1 cup light cream
¼ teaspoon salt
Cayenne
1 cup finely-diced Cheddar cheese
A few drops puréed garlic
½ can (4½-oz. size) minced ripe
  olives (about ⅓ cup)
4 eggs, separated

Melt butter, add flour, and blend over heat. Add cream, salt, and a dash of cayenne, and cook until thickened and smooth. Stir in cheese, garlic, and ripe olives. Continue cooking and stirring until the cheese is melted, then remove from the heat and add well-beaten egg yolks. Thirty-five minutes before serving, beat egg whites until stiff but still shiny and smooth, and fold them into the cheese mixture—they do not have to be incorporated too thoroughly. Bake in a moderate oven (350°) for 35 minutes, and serve at once. Makes 6 to 8 servings.

Curried Scrambled Eggs

Try these for lunch, with rice and chutney, and serve fruit for dessert.

For 8 or 9 eggs, cook 2 tablespoons chopped onion in ⅓ cup butter or margarine until golden. Stir in 2 teaspoons curry powder, cover, and cook for 3 minutes. In the meantime, beat eggs slightly with 1 teaspoon salt and 2 tablespoons cream. Pour into onion mixture and scramble as usual over low heat until just set. Makes 6 servings.

California Omelette

This makes a good luncheon dish, served with crisp bacon and corn bread.

Dice 1 ripe avocado; peel 1 large tomato, cut in half, gently press out the seeds, and dice. Melt 3 tablespoons butter or margarine in a skillet, add 1 cup sliced fresh mushrooms, and cook for 5 minutes, along with 1 tablespoon minced shallots or green onions.

Add the tomato, cook for 1 minute, sprinkle with salt, pepper, and a little chopped dill (optional), then add the avocado. Turn off heat and keep covered while you make two individual 3-egg omelettes, using half of the filling in each omelette before folding. Makes 2 servings.

Eggs with Eggplant

These eggs cook on top of eggplant slices, with a flavorful tomato sauce over all.

Heat 1 small clove of mashed or puréed garlic in 1 tablespoon olive oil. Add 4 peeled, seeded, and chopped fresh tomatoes, 2 teaspoons minced parsley, and salt and pepper to taste. Simmer for half an hour. Slice 1 unpeeled eggplant about ⅜-inch thick, dip in seasoned flour, and sauté in ¼ cup salad oil (part olive oil for flavor) until brown on one side. Turn, break 1 egg on each slice of eggplant (you'll need 6 or 8 eggs). Cover and continue cooking until the eggs are set. Remove to a hot platter, pour on the hot sauce, and sprinkle with parsley. Makes 6 to 8 servings.

Egg Fromage Verte et Rouge

This cold egg dish is nice for a summer lunch, with green salad and a hot bread.

Oil a small (6 to 6½-inch) ring mold and carefully break in 8 eggs. Place in a larger pan, filled with boiling water, and bake in a moderate oven (350°) for 15 minutes, or until just set. The eggs should not be hard cooked. Cool, turn out on a round plate, mask with Sauce Verte, and fill center with Sauce Rouge. Makes 4 servings.

Sauce Verte: Whirl together in a blender ⅔ cup mayonnaise and 1 tablespoon each chopped chives, parsley, tarragon, and chervil.

Sauce Rouge: Mix together 1 cup mayonnaise, a good dash of liquid hot-pepper seasoning, and ¼ cup tomato purée. Add salt to taste.

Oeufs mollets is the French name for eggs that are dropped into boiling water, simmered for 5 minutes, plunged into cold water for a few seconds, then shelled. You can use these eggs in many interesting ways. To serve as a first course or a supper dish, put each egg in a small baked pastry shell—preferably oval—then mask with Hollandaise, mushroom, Mornay, or herb sauce, and serve hot, at once.

Huevos con Salsa Aguacates

These eggs are served with an avocado sauce.

Hard cook and peel 8 eggs, and keep in hot water while preparing this sauce: Cook 2 tablespoons minced onion in 2 tablespoons butter until wilted; add 1 minced canned green chili pepper, 1 tablespoon flour, and ½ cup milk. Cook until thick (this can be done ahead of time). Press the flesh of 2 ripe avocados through a sieve, or whirl in a blender. Add the hot sauce, season with salt to taste, and pour over the hot eggs (which have been drained); put in a serving dish.

Eggs à la Parmentier

This makes a pleasantly inexpensive and appetizing main dish. If you are short of time, you can build the potato rim with a spoon instead of using a pastry bag.

Scrub 3 large potatoes and bake until tender. Cool slightly, cut in halves, and carefully scoop out the centers, leaving a quarter-inch wall. Have ready 1½ cups Béchamel Sauce (page 152) or cream sauce, 6 small poached eggs, and 2 tablespoons grated Parmesan or Romano cheese. Combine ½ cup of the sauce with the potato and mash smooth. Season to taste and line the potato shells with half of this mixture. Trim eggs if they are ragged, and slip one into each potato shell.

Add cheese to the remaining potato and, using a pastry bag and star tube, pipe a ½-inch rim around each potato. Fill center with the remaining sauce and bake in a moderately hot oven (375°) until the tops are gold-flecked. Makes 6 servings.

Shrimp Chow Dun

This is a very easy-to-prepare Chinese egg dish. A similar dish, Chawan-mushi, is served in Japan.

1 cup diced raw shrimp
½ cup each canned sliced mushrooms, chopped onion, and thawed frozen peas (uncooked)
2 tablespoons salad oil
8 eggs
¼ teaspoon monosodium glutamate
½ teaspoon salt
Pepper

Cook shrimp and vegetables for 3 minutes in heated oil in a frying pan (the Chinese would use a *wok*). To the eggs, add monosodium glutamate, salt, and some pepper; beat just enough to mix. Pour eggs over the vegetables, distributing them as evenly as possible. Turn heat very low, and cook just until the eggs begin to set. They should be moist and creamy. Serve at once. Makes 6 servings.

Huevos en Toledo

Here's a dish that is typically Spanish, using eggs, olive oil, ham, and pimientos.

1 cup chopped cooked ham
1 tablespoon ham fat or olive oil
2 cups cooked peas
2 canned pimientos, chopped
¼ cup chopped green olives
Salt and pepper, if needed
6 eggs
2 tablespoons olive oil

Sauté ham in ham fat or olive oil for 2 or 3 minutes. Combine with peas, pimiento, and olives. Heat well and add salt and pepper, if necessary. Put in the middle of a hot platter and surround with the eggs, which have been slowly fried in the 2 tablespoons olive oil. Makes 6 servings.

Eggs Mayonnaise with Shrimps

This is a favorite Swedish way with eggs. It is frequently included in Easter Eve supper, at which the Swedish people eat eggs prepared in at least three ways.

Cook 2 pounds shelled, medium-sized, green shrimps in salted water for 4 minutes. Drain and remove sand veins. Hard cook 6 eggs, cut them in halves crosswise, and slice a tiny bit from the bottoms so they will stand straight. Put in the middle of a round platter and surround with the shrimp, arranging them symmetrically.

Combine ¾ cup mayonnaise and ½ cup heavy cream, whipped, and pour over the eggs. Garnish the shrimps with feathery sprigs of fresh dill, if you can find it, or with parsley. Sprinkle chopped chives on the eggs. Makes 6 servings.

Eggs with Tuna Sauce

This is a luncheon dish, special enough to serve to guests.

Cut 3 large tomatoes in half and gently squeeze out and discard the seeds. Brush with melted butter and broil until lightly browned but still firm. In the meantime, butter 6 individual baking dishes (small glass pie pans or soufflé dishes are ideal).) Arrange about 2 tablespoons of cooked rice on the bottom of each dish, top with the tomato, and then with a poached egg. Pour over the tuna sauce (below), garnish with a feather of parsley or dill, and serve at once.

Tuna Sauce: Combine 1 can (7 oz.) tuna chunks, drained, with 1½ cups thin cream sauce. Season with 1 teaspoon lemon juice and salt and pepper to taste.

Try serving spreadable cheeses with crusty French bread instead of with crackers, as a separate course after the entrée or salad. Sweet butter, too, goes well with cheeses, particularly blue or Gorgonzola or a very sharp Cheddar.

Tortillas con Hongos

Tortillas with mushrooms and eggs are a delicious combination.

Wash and chop ½ pound mushrooms, stems and all. Put in a skillet with ½ cup finely minced onion and 1 pressed clove of garlic (optional), and cook in 3 tablespoons butter or shortening for 10 minutes. Add 4 beaten eggs, ½ teaspoon salt, a little pepper, and ½ cup finely diced jack cheese. Cook, stirring, until the eggs are set but still soft. Serve on crisply fried tortillas. Makes 4 servings.

Fonduta

This is the Italian version of cheese fondue. It depends upon truffles for its distinctive flavor.

Shred 1 pound Fontina cheese (or 4 oz. Bel Paese and 12 oz. Mozzarella). Cover with 1 cup milk and let it stand in the refrigerator overnight or longer. Put in the top of a double boiler over hot, not boiling, water and cook, stirring occasionally, until the cheese is melted and smooth. Add ¼ cup butter and 4 slightly beaten egg yolks, and continue cooking over the hot water until thick and smooth. (On rare instances, the cheese gets temperamental and forms a solid plastic lump; this can be whirled smooth in the blender.)

Season to taste with salt and pepper, and add a very thinly sliced truffle. (White truffles from northern Italy are traditional, but if you can't find them, use a black one and ½ small clove of garlic, puréed.) Keep warm while serving, either in an earthenware fondue pot, a chafing dish with a water jacket, or in the double boiler. Serve with crusty pieces of bread to be speared on fondue forks, then dipped in the fonduta, or with crispy bread sticks that serve the same purpose admirably.

A subtle change in cheese flavor is apparent to persons with very well developed palates. They claim, with complete sincerity, that cheese in chunks tastes better than cheese that is thinly sliced. Can you detect the difference?

Cheese and Spinach Quiche

This is good served with baked ham or sliced smoked tongue, and is fine for a buffet.

Line a 9-inch pan with pastry (your own recipe or a prepared mix). Place another pan of the same size inside it and bake in a moderately hot oven (375°) for 10 minutes. Remove from oven, take off top pan, and cool.

Cook 4 minced shallots or green onions in 2 tablespoons butter until wilted. Combine with 1 cup finely chopped, *very* well drained cooked spinach, 3 slightly beaten eggs, 1½ cups light cream, ½ teaspoon salt, a dash of freshly grated nutmeg, a grinding or two of pepper. Pour into the pastry shell, sprinkle with ¼ cup shredded Gruyère cheese, dot with tiny pieces of butter (about 1 tablespoon total), and bake in a moderately hot oven (375°) for 30 minutes, or until the filling is set and the top brown. Makes 6 servings.

Ajoqueso

Here is a garlicky version of Mexican *chili con queso* (chili with cheese). It can be made in a chafing dish or electric frying pan at the table, and served over toast or toasted corn or wheat tortillas. (Ajoqueso is also good served with corn chips as an appetizer.)

Rinse the seeds from 1 small can (4 oz.) peeled green chilies and cut into small dice. Mince 1 large onion and 2 cloves garlic and cook them in ¼ cup olive oil until wilted. Add 2 tablespoons flour, and stir over heat for 2 minutes, then gradually stir in 1 cup light cream; stir until smooth. Add ½ pound shredded mild Cheddar or jack cheese and the chilies. Heat, stirring until cheese melts. Makes about 4 servings.

Fish & Shellfish

Fish and shellfish are versatile foods. Depending on their sauces, seasonings, or the ingredients with which they are combined, they may change character completely. Crab, in one recipe, is used in simple fish cakes, in another as a hearty main dish casserole. The delicate flavor of sole is equally compatible with eggplant or with cucumber.

Fish is considerably less popular in most American homes than are meat and poultry. One reason for this indifference may be that fish is so frequently overcooked. It is a fragile food, with a delicate flavor—actually many differing flavors, because our waters teem with a huge variety of fish. Foreigners treat fish more kindly, demanding really fresh ones and cooking them so they retain all of their moisture, tenderness, and flavor. Here we have borrowed from those experts, and we have also come up with ideas of our own—new ways to vary fish and shellfish with interesting seasonings and sauces. With these recipes as a guide, and with a little bold experimentation, the enthusiastic cook should be able to produce some veritable works of art that will be welcomed with enthusiasm by all who sample them.

Crab and Hominy Casserole

Here's a colorful and delicious main dish casserole.

Drain a large can (1 lb., 13 oz.) whole hominy, and cook until golden in 3 tablespoons of butter. Add 1 pound flaked crab meat, 1 can (4 oz.) sliced ripe olives, 2 tablespoons each diced canned pimientos and green chilies, 2 cups cream sauce, and salt and pepper to taste. Put into a casserole, top with buttered crumbs, and bake in a moderate oven (350°) until brown, about 20 minutes. Makes 6 servings.

Crab Cakes

Fish cakes of crab meat make a dish fit for the fanciest luncheon.

Cook 2 tablespoons minced shallots or green onions in 1 tablespoon butter. Combine with 1 pound crab meat, 1 cup mashed potatoes, 1 beaten egg, and ½ teaspoon salt. Form into 8 oval cakes, dust very lightly with flour, and sauté in butter or margarine until brown on both sides. Serve garnished with lemon halves and sprigs of watercress. Makes 8 servings.

Frogs' Legs à la Poulette

This is fine for a chafing dish.

Poach 1 pound of frogs' legs for 4 or 5 minutes in ¾ cup dry white wine. Drain them, reserving liquid. Heat together 1 cup of the liquid in which frogs' legs were cooked and 1 cup light cream; thicken with a roux made by blending 3 tablespoons each butter and flour. Whisk in 2 egg yolks and 1 tablespoon minced parsley. Reheat frogs' legs in the sauce, but do not allow to boil. Serve with toast points. Makes 4 servings.

Prawns with Cream

This is a good one for the chafing dish or electric skillet.

Cook 2 pounds large raw shrimp or prawns in court bouillon for 5 minutes. Drain, peel, and de-vein. Heat ¼ cup butter in the chafing dish or electric skillet, add shrimp, and brown lightly. Add ¼ cup cognac or sherry, ½ cup cream, 1 tablespoon minced parsley, and salt and pepper to taste. Heat well and serve with pastry squares or toast. Makes 6 servings.

The bayous of the south-central part of Louisiana abound with crawfish, and Breaux Bridge, a town about 30 miles north of New Iberia calls itself "The Crawfish Capital of the World." The shellfish are caught by Cajuns who go out at night in pirogues or panisses (boats fashioned from logs or planks) to set their net-like traps. If fishing is good, the nets will be filled by morning with the shrimp-like creatures, averaging about three inches in length, which the Cajuns sell to local restaurants or send to New Orleans.

Truite au Bleu

Fresh-caught trout are cooked this way in many of the world's finest restaurants. The fish will not turn a proper blue unless they are just out of the water—the restaurants keep tanks of live trout, but in season, the fisherman can flip a trout directly from the water to the pot, provided, of course, he can hook the fish.

Prepare a pot of simmering court bouillon before you catch your fish. To make 1 quart, simmer together 1 cup vinegar, 3 cups water, ½ bay leaf, 5 peppercorns, and 1 teaspoon salt. Kill your wriggling fish with a blow on the back of the head, clean it *at once,* and plunge it into the simmering court bouillon. The average trout will cook in 4 minutes. Serve at once with melted butter, and with boiled potatoes, if you wish.

Scallop Seviche

This Mexican dish, served icy cold in nests of lettuce, is ideal as a first course. Heaped into avocado halves or scooped-out tomatoes, it makes a pleasant addition to a buffet.

Cut into small dice or coarsely chop 1 pound raw scallops. Cover with fresh lemon or lime juice; cover dish, and let stand in the refrigerator for a couple of hours or until scallops lose their translucence. Drain well and mix with 2 ripe tomatoes that have been peeled, seeded, and cut in small dice, 4 to 6 finely chopped green onions, and 1 firm but ripe avocado, cut in dice. Season to taste with salt. Makes 8 servings.

Scandinavian Fish Scallop

This distinctive luncheon dish requires surprisingly little effort; simply combine canned crab meat and fish balls with a rich cream sauce, and bake. The Scandinavian canned fish balls are very much like the famous fish quenelles of France.

2 tablespoons minced green onions or shallots
4 tablespoons (¼ cup) butter
¼ cup flour
2 cups light cream or milk
1 can (8 oz.) crab meat
3 tablespoons capers
Salt and pepper to taste
1 can (1 lb.) Danish or Norwegian fish balls
1 cup cracker crumbs
2 tablespoons melted butter

Cook onion in the 4 tablespoons butter until wilted; add flour and cook for 1 minute. Gradually stir in milk, and cook slowly, stirring, until sauce thickens. Add crab meat, capers, salt, and pepper. Add fish balls (if they are the large ones, cut them in half), and pour into a 1-quart baking dish. Or divide the mixture in individual scallop shells. Sprinkle top with cracker crumbs mixed with the 2 tablespoons melted butter. Heat in a hot oven (400°) until the mixture is bubbly and the top is browned. Makes about 6 servings.

Escabeche de Pescado

Like *seviche*, this is a Mexican recipe for pickled or "soused" fish, but the fish for *escabeche* is cooked over heat whereas that for seviche is cooked only by the action of the acid in the lemon or lime juice. Also, escabeche may be fish, tongue, brains, or many other things, while seviche is always fish or shellfish.

2 pounds fish steak
½ cup olive oil
1 large onion, sliced
2 whole cloves garlic
2 canned green chilies, chopped
½ cup vinegar
¼ teaspoon cumin
1 teaspoon salt
Juice of 1 orange
Lettuce, sliced oranges, ripe olives, and sliced hard-cooked eggs for garnish

Sauté fish steak in olive oil on both sides until lightly browned. Arrange in a shallow dish. In the same pan, cook onion and garlic cloves (thread them on a toothpick) until lightly browned. Discard garlic; add chilies, vinegar, cumin, salt, and orange juice. Pour over the fish and chill. Serve garnished with lettuce, sliced oranges, ripe olives, and sliced hard-cooked eggs. Makes 8 servings.

Fresh Albacore

Fishermen's wives are often nonplused when they face an albacore that they are expected to cook. Here's a good way to cook this fish.

Cut the albacore in steaks, discarding both skin and the black fat that lies near the spine (this fat has an especially fishy flavor and is best removed before cooking). Put the slices in a well-buttered baking dish. For each 2 pounds of fish, pour on 1 cup each white wine and tomato juice; sprinkle the fish with a mixture of 1 cup bread crumbs, 1 pressed clove garlic, ¼ cup melted butter, and ¼ cup parsley. Sprinkle with salt and pepper, and bake in a hot oven (400°) for 15 minutes, or until the flesh separates easily when pierced with a fork.

Crayfish or Shrimp à la Bordelaise

As practically every good cook knows, a dish labeled *Bordelaise* is from the Bordeaux region of France, and usually contains some Bordeaux wine. Not always, though; sometimes it qualifies because it is made with the *cèpes* (a delicate fungus) of the region, or because it is garnished with artichokes, or simply because it contains a *mirepoix*, as in this recipe. Serve this with crusty bread, and supply your guests with large napkins or bibs.

1 large carrot
1 medium-sized onion
2 ribs celery
¼ cup butter
Small pinch thyme
½ bay leaf
Salt and pepper to taste
About 30 crayfish, or about 30 large shrimp or prawns
¼ cup cognac
2 cups white Bordeaux or any dry white wine
3 egg yolks (or 1½ tablespoons each flour and butter, kneaded together)

Make a *mirepoix* by mincing the carrot, onion, and celery. Put in a heavy pan with the butter, thyme, and bay leaf, and cook very slowly until the vegetables are tender. Discard bay leaf and season with salt and pepper.

Wash crayfish well; from each crayfish pull the tiny wing in the center of the tail, and the black vein. (Or wash shrimp or prawns; split shells down the back with scissors, remove sand veins, but leave shells on.) Warm cognac, pour over crayfish or shrimp, and set aflame. When the flames die down, add the mirepoix and the wine. Cover and cook for 10 minutes. Drain, saving the sauce.

Put the crayfish or shrimp in a deep platter and keep warm while binding the sauce with the egg yolks or the flour and butter mixture. Correct seasoning, pour over crayfish, and serve.

Norwegian Fish Pudding

Soufflé-like fish pudding makes a delightful luncheon dish. It's also excellent as a first or fish course at a rather formal dinner. You can use halibut, red snapper, sole, or any firm white fish.

Make a thick cream sauce with 6 tablespoons butter, 6 tablespoons flour, 2 teaspoons salt, some freshly ground black pepper, and 2 cups milk. Cut 1½ pounds raw, boneless fish into small pieces. Put half the sauce and half the fish into an electric blender and whirl smooth; repeat with remainder. (Or grind the fish, force it through a food mill, and combine with the cream sauce.) Beat 6 egg yolks until thick, and add to the fish mixture; beat the 6 egg whites until stiff and mix in carefully.

Pour mixture into a well-greased, 1½-quart casserole, set in a larger pan containing 1 inch of hot water. Bake in a moderate oven (350°) for 1 hour, or until set and slightly brown. Serve with melted butter, Hollandaise (page 151), or dill sauce. (For a quick dill sauce, combine 1 cup sour cream, 1 cup mayonnaise, 1 tablespoon dill weed, and 1 teaspoon lemon juice, and whirl in the blender.) Makes 6 servings.

Many people roast turkey with an oyster stuffing, or garnish the bird with bacon-wrapped oysters. Here's another way to use oysters with turkey: Pour off the drippings from the roasting pan and skim, as usual, for the gravy. Pour ½ cup of the surplus fat into a skillet and heat. Simmer 1 cup of small oysters in the fat until the edges curl. Drain oysters well and add to the gravy.

Oysters à la Benedict

A good hearty breakfast dish, or a luncheon dish, is Oysters à la Benedict.

Split and toast English muffins, cover with a slice of cooked ham and some drained poached oysters, then mask with Hollandaise sauce (page 151). (To poach oysters, cook them in their own juices until the edges curl.)

Oysters Mignonette

A classic sauce for oysters is called mignonette. It's peppery, but lots of people like strong flavors with this shellfish.

Crush ½ cup white peppercorns in a mortar, or on a board with a rolling pin. It shouldn't be too fine. Add 4 finely minced shallots or green onions, 1 tablespoon minced chives, 1 teaspoon salt, and 1 cup tarragon vinegar. Serve in small glasses, or in cups made from small green peppers, placing the sauce in the middle of the plates, and surrounding with raw oysters in the half shell (or arrange shucked oysters for each serving on a scallop or other shell). Sauce is enough for 8 to 10 servings.

Fillet of Sole with Eggplant

No other vegetable is necessary when you serve this fish dish. Crisp shoestring potatoes make a very compatible garnish.

1 large can (1 lb., 13 oz.) tomatoes
1 onion, sliced
1 clove garlic, crushed
1 tablespoon chopped fat ham or lean bacon
Herb bouquet
Salt and pepper to taste
1 small can (2 oz.) sliced pimientos
1 large eggplant
Salt
Shortening
6 fillets of sole
Seasoned flour

In a saucepan, combine the tomatoes, onion, garlic, ham, and herb bouquet; cook until reduced one-half. Whirl in a blender or force through a sieve. Season to taste with salt and pepper. (If the sauce is too thin, add a small amount of *beurre manie*—butter and flour in equal parts, kneaded together—and cook until thickened.) Add pimientos.

Cut eggplant lengthwise into 6 slices, discarding outside pieces. Sprinkle with salt and let stand for 30 minutes, then drain and dry. Sauté in shortening until lightly browned on both sides. Remove to a platter and keep warm. Dip fillets of sole in seasoned flour; sauté in the same pan. When nicely browned, place 1 fillet on each eggplant slice, and cover with the hot tomato sauce. Makes 6 servings.

Fillet of Sole with Cucumbers

This is an unusual and delicious way to serve sole.

Salt and pepper 2 pounds fish fillets and dust lightly with flour. Cook gently in ¼ cup butter or margarine. In another pan cook 2 peeled thinly sliced cucumbers in additional ¼ cup butter or margarine. Cover the pan so that the cucumbers become transparent. Put fish on a hot platter, surround with cucumbers, sprinkle with parsley, and pour over a sauce made by combining the juices in the two pans and adding 2 tablespoons lemon juice. Makes 6 to 8 servings.

Salmon and Green Olive Casserole

This casserole, made from canned salmon, has enough distinction to star at a buffet.

- 2 tablespoons chopped shallots or green onions
- ¼ cup butter
- ¼ flour
- Freshly ground pepper
- 1 can (1 lb.) salmon
- Light cream
- ½ cup green olives, cut from their pits and diced
- 2 teaspoons dill weed
- Salt (if needed)
- 3 tablespoons buttered crumbs

Sauté shallots or green onions in butter until wilted. Drain salmon, saving liquid. To the pan in which onions were cooked add the flour, about 2 grindings of pepper, and the salmon liquid combined with enough cream to make 2 cups of liquid. Cook, stirring, until thick and smooth. Add olives, dill weed, and salt if necessary. Remove skin from the salmon; break salmon into large pieces and place in a 1-quart casserole. Pour in the sauce, turn 2 or 3 times with a fork to mix, and sprinkle top with the buttered crumbs. Before serving, heat in a hot oven (400°) for 15 minutes, or until hot and brown. Makes 6 servings.

Koulibiak

This Russian specialty is a large turnover made of rich yeast pastry; it can be filled with meat, fish, hard-cooked eggs, rice or kasha—or a combination. Choux paste or brioche dough is sometimes used for the crust, but this recipe is for the traditional kind used in Russia in the days of the czars.

1 package yeast (active dry or compressed)
¼ cup warm water (lukewarm for compressed yeast)
¼ cup scalded milk, cooled to lukewarm
About 2½ cups sifted flour
3 eggs
½ cup (¼ pound) soft butter
¼ teaspoon salt
2 pounds salmon fillets (cut from the tail end)
2 tablespoons butter
1 tablespoon lemon juice
2 tablespoons minced parsley
2 teaspoons dill weed
Salt to taste
3 cups cooked rice, kasha, or cracked wheat, seasoned with salt to taste and ¼ cup melted butter
3 hard-cooked eggs, sliced thin
1 egg, slightly beaten
Melted butter or sour cream

Dissolve yeast in the warm water. Stir in the scalded and cooled milk. Add 1 cup of the flour, and allow to rise until doubled in bulk. Add the 3 eggs, the ½ cup soft butter, the remaining 1½ cups flour, and the ¼ teaspoon salt. Beat well and long, preferably with an electric mixer. Allow to rise again, then turn out on a floured board and work in enough more flour to make a soft but not sticky dough.

For the filling, sauté salmon fillets in the 2 tablespoons butter until lightly browned. Sprinkle with lemon juice and allow to cool. Chop about ½ pound of the cooked salmon; add parsley and dill weed. Season with salt to taste and reserve.

Roll out pastry in a rectangle about 12 by 18 inches. Roll onto the pin, then unroll on a lightly floured cloth or piece of heavy foil. Spread the center of the rectangle with the chopped salmon, cover with half the rice or kasha, and arrange the salmon fillets over it. Cover with the sliced eggs, sprinkle with salt and pepper, and top with the remaining rice. Fold edges and ends of pastry over the filling and press together tightly to seal. Put a buttered baking sheet upside down on the pastry, and turn over, cloth or foil and all. Remove cloth, slash pastry, and brush with the slightly beaten egg. Bake in a moderately hot oven (375°) for 35 minutes, or until nicely browned. Slice and serve with melted butter or sour cream. Makes 6 servings.

Lobster à l'Americaine

This is superb and not difficult to make. In France it's usually made with *homard*, the large clawed lobster of the Atlantic, but the Pacific's *langouste* is often used. In either case, the lobster should be fresh, which means it should be purchased alive. This takes a bit of doing unless you live near the coast, and even then you will probably have to order them in advance. However, the time and trouble involved in getting live lobsters will be worth it.

2 lobsters, 2 to 2½ pounds each (or 3 lobsters, 1½ to 2 pounds each)
½ cup olive oil
½ cup (¼ pound) butter
4 shallots or green onions, chopped
1 large onion, chopped
1 clove garlic, puréed
2 cups dry white table wine
2 pounds tomatoes, peeled, seeded, and chopped
2 teaspoons each salt and tarragon
½ teaspoon thyme
½ bay leaf
⅓ cup cognac
¼ cup minced parsley

To kill lobster, put point of a heavy knife on the lobster head, between the eyes, and hit with a mallet—or simply split the head if you are strong enough. Then cut the tail in crosswise slices, making the cuts in the natural divisions of the shell. Also cut the meat from the body (there is more in a *langouste* than in an *homard*), including shell when possible. Reserve liver (the yellow part) and, if there is any, the coral or roe (pale or deep pink). Also save the juice, which is blood; discard intestines.

Heat olive oil and butter in a heavy saucepan. When hot, add the lobster—meat, shells, and all. Cook quickly until the meat barely loses its transparent look. (Don't overcook!)

Remove the lobster. To the pan add the shallots, onion, and garlic, and cook until onion is wilted. Add wine, tomatoes, salt, tarragon, thyme, and bay leaf, and simmer together for 25 minutes. Heat cognac, pour over the lobster, and flame. When the flames die down, add the lobster and the blood to the sauce. Simmer, covered, for 15 minutes; chop the coral and the liver, and add. Heat, correct seasoning, discard bay leaf, and pour into a deep platter. (The shells may be removed at this point, if you prefer.) Sprinkle with parsley. Makes 6 servings.

Meats

This chapter runs the gamut from the most simple of recipes to others that take the time an interested cook loves to lavish on a new and interesting dish. You'll find the usual roasts of beef, pork, or lamb, but not the usual ways of cooking them. Even the lowly meat ball takes on grandeur here. There are classic recipes, some from foreign lands, some that are entirely new. There are recipes for both expensive and inexpensive cuts, and for innards, and a few recipes that make good use of leftovers. Some use wines or herbs or both for accent, and some are deliciously sauced; others rely solely on the flavor of the meat itself.

We don't have space to go into the importance of meat grades, cuts, aging, or even cooking in general, and this is not that kind of cook book. What we hope we have done is to present enough different recipes for meat to make it obvious that there is no end to marvelous ways of cooking it, and no excuse for meat dishes becoming monotonous.

In many of these recipes, the meats are interchangeable, which in itself should be a good way to explore new directions and to discover recipes that will be your very own.

Tenderloin Steak Casanova

The next time you feel like splurging, impress your guests with this outstanding steak dish.

Brush 1-inch-thick tenderloin steaks with olive oil, then sprinkle with salt and pepper. Let stand while you ready a charcoal fire and prepare this sauce: Heat 4 ounces *pâté de foie gras* with ¼ cup cream sherry or Marsala in a large frying pan, stirring until smooth. Broil the steaks to your liking, then put in the frying pan on top of the sauce. Add ¼ cup warm cognac, then flame. As the burning cognac blends with the sauce, spoon it over the steaks and serve at once. Sauce is enough for 6 servings.

Chinese Beef with Oyster Sauce

One of the most delectable Chinese dishes depends upon oyster sauce for its distinction. The sauce comes in bottles and is available in Chinese markets. It keeps indefinitely when refrigerated, and can add flavor to many dishes, Occidental and Oriental.

1 pound lean beef (sirloin, round, or rump), sliced very thin
1 piece fresh ginger (about 1 by 1½ inches)
2 tablespoons soy sauce
2 tablespoons cognac
1 tablespoon cornstarch
1 clove garlic, crushed
1 tablespoon salad oil
3 tablespoons oyster sauce
1 cup water

Cut meat into strips. Scrape and grate ginger; mix ginger with soy sauce, cognac, and cornstarch. Add meat and toss well together; allow to stand for 1 hour. Heat garlic in oil; add meat and cook quickly, stirring, for 2 minutes. Add oyster sauce and cook for another 30 seconds, then pour in water. Cook, still stirring, until the sauce thickens and clears. Serve at once with rice. Makes about 4 servings.

Steak au Poivre

In France, *steak au poivre*, or pepper steak, is a great favorite. The pepper is coarsely ground black pepper, which is pressed in liberal amounts on both sides of the raw steak. The steak is then cooked quickly and flamed with cognac. This is a good dish to prepare at the table in an electric skillet.

Have a "minute" steak for each person—a ½-inch-thick club steak is perfect. Coarsely crush some peppercorns with a rolling pin (if you put them in a paper bag first, you'll have no trouble) and press them into both sides of the steak with your hands—about 1 teaspoon to a steak. Have the skillet hot. For 3 steaks, sauté 2 minced shallots or green onions in 2 tablespoons beef fat or salad oil. When the shallots are tender, push to one side and add the steaks. Cook quickly on one side, turn and cook the other. When the steaks are done to your liking, pour in about 3 ounces of cognac and ignite. As soon as the flames die down, put steaks on hot plates and add 3 tablespoons red wine, cream, or bouillon to the pan. Scrape up pan crispings and ladle over steaks.

Herbed hamburgers have long been popular. For a change, though, why not make herbed buns to serve with plain hamburgers? To a package of hot roll mix, add ½ cup each chopped onions and parsley, 2 teaspoons salt, ½ teaspoon pepper, and 2 teaspoons fresh marjoram. Form into round buns.

Creamed Beef and Avocado

Here's a breakfast dish that's special enough to serve at a party brunch, yet easy enough to make for the family as a weekday treat.

Tear ¼ pound of dried beef into pieces and cook in ¼ cup butter until slightly frizzled. Stir in 3 tablespoons flour, 2 cups milk, 1 bouillon cube, and salt and pepper to taste. Cook until smooth and thick. Keep warm while making 6 pieces of toast and peeling and slicing 1 large avocado. Arrange sliced avocado on toast, and over this pour the creamed dried beef. Another avocado may be sliced and used as a garnish, if desired. Makes 6 servings.

Kafta ala Sheesh

These are broiled meat balls from Arabia. The Arabs serve them in a split loaf of bread.

Combine 2 pounds thrice-ground beef or lamb, 2 teaspoons salt, a few grindings of black pepper (about ½ teaspoon), 1 cup finely minced onions, and 1 cup minced parsley. Form into balls about 1 inch in diameter and thread on 8 skewers (this should make 6 for each skewer). Brush with olive oil and cook over charcoal until brown on all sides. Serve with yogurt as a sauce. Makes 8 servings.

Arab Meat Balls with Pine Nut Sauce

This is similar to Kafta ala Sheesh, above, but in this version the meat balls are fried in butter and sauced instead of being skewered and broiled, and the onion is added to the sauce instead of to the meat.

Mix 2 pounds thrice-ground beef or lamb with 2 teaspoons salt, a few grindings of black pepper, and 1 cup minced parsley. Form into balls about 1 inch in diameter and sauté in ½ cup butter or shortening until brown. Transfer meat balls to a dish and keep warm. To the pan, add 1 cup finely minced onions and ½ cup shelled pine nuts, and brown. Add 2 tablespoons tomato paste and 2½ cups water. Simmer for 5 minutes and serve on the meat balls. Makes 8 servings.

Chirrasquillas

This interesting main dish from Costa Rica is made with tortillas and ground meat. Costa Ricans serve it with a garnish of fried plantains; you could use green bananas, sliced and fried in the same fat. Refried beans and fried chorizo sausages are good accompaniments.

1 large onion, chopped
2 tablespoons lard or shortening
1 pound ground beef
1 teaspoon salt
Pepper
Oregano
1 small clove garlic, puréed
12 tortillas
1 cup beer or water
1 cup flour
½ teaspoon salt
3 eggs

Sauté onion in lard or shortening until wilted. Add ground beef, salt, a dash of pepper, a pinch of oregano, and garlic. Cook until the meat browns, mashing with a fork to dispel lumps. Cool and divide the mixture among the tortillas, spooning some of the mixture into the center of each. Fold over as you would turnovers, and fasten with toothpicks.

Make a batter by beating together the beer, flour, salt, and eggs. Dip the folded tortillas into batter, one at a time, and fry in deep fat at 365° to 370° or in 1½ inches salad oil in a large frying pan. Serve with a Spanish-style hot tomato sauce.

Beef Lindstrom

This comes from Sweden. It is merely glorified hamburger, but well worth adding to your repertoire. Serve it at any meal—breakfast, lunch, or dinner.

Combine 1½ pounds very finely ground lean beef with 1 cup finely diced cooked potatoes, 1 cup finely diced cooked beets, 1½ teaspoons salt, a little pepper, 2 tablespoons minced onion, and 1 tablespoon minced capers. Form into flat patties and brown on both sides in butter. Top each with a butter-fried egg. Makes 6 servings.

Mexican Stuffed Roast

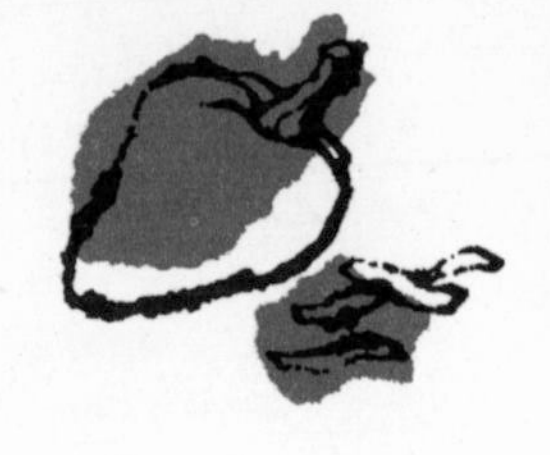

This is unusual, and it's as attractive as it is flavorful.

4 or 5-pound rolled roast of beef
1 onion
1 green pepper
2 whole pimientos
½ pound ham
1 clove garlic
2 tablespoons wine vinegar
2 teaspoons salt
½ teaspoon oregano
Pepper
Stuffed olives
1 can (8 oz.) tomato sauce
½ cup bouillon

With a strong sharp knife, make large deep holes all over the top of the roast (placing roast with the cords around the side). Grind together the onion, green pepper, pimientos, ham, and garlic. Add vinegar, salt, oregano, and a little pepper, and mix together thoroughly. Stuff holes in meat with this mixture, and plug each hole with a stuffed olive. Let stand, refrigerated, for at least 12 hours. Put in a roasting pan with the tomato sauce, any left-over stuffing mixture, and the bouillon. Roast in a moderate oven (350°) until done to your liking. (Use a meat thermometer.)

Carbonnade of Beef

A good beef stew is always welcome. This one is classically made with beer, but if you wish, you can substitute consommé or tomato juice. Serve it with noodles or mashed potatoes.

3 pounds boneless shoulder of beef, cut in 1-inch cubes
½ cup flour
1 tablespoon salt
Freshly ground pepper
3 large onions, sliced
⅓ cup shortening
1 clove garlic, crushed
2 cups beer (or consommé or tomato juice)
Herb bouquet (thyme, parsley, and bay)
Minced parsley

Dredge meat in flour that has been seasoned with the salt and pepper. Cook onions in shortening until wilted; remove and reserve. To the same pan, add garlic and the meat, and brown thoroughly. Add the onions, beer, and herb bouquet. Cover and simmer for 1¼ hours, or until tender. Correct seasonings, discard herb bouquet, and serve sprinkled with minced parsley. Makes 6 generous servings.

Fondue Bourguignonne

Fondue means, to most of us, a dish of melted cheese. But in Burgundy, land of great wines and great food, they make another kind, with beef and melted butter. It is truly an adventure in food. It may be served as the main course at a dinner for 4 or 6, or as an hors d'oeuvre at a larger party (provide each guest with a small plate to hold the anchovy butter and prevent disastrous dripping).

Cut 2 pounds tenderloin of beef into ½-inch cubes. Drain a 2-ounce tin of anchovy fillets and mash fillets in a mortar to a paste. Add 2 tablespoons olive oil, ½ teaspoon paprika, ¼ pound softened butter or margarine, and ⅛ teaspoon freshly ground pepper, and mix well. (Or whirl ingredients smooth in a blender.) Refrigerate the butter until serving time. To serve as a main dish, give each guest a small bowl of the butter and a bowl of the raw meat. Have ½ pound hot melted butter in a chafing dish, or an earthenware casserole over a warmer, in the center of the table. Each guest spears a cube of beef, whirls it around in the bubbling butter until it's done to his liking, dips it in the anchovy butter, and eats it piping hot. Serve some crusty French bread with the fondue. This serves 6 as a main dish, or about 16 as an hors d'oeuvre.

Bata Yaki

This delicious Japanese dish is very like sukiyaki, but much simpler. To suit the American taste for rare beef, we reverse the Japanese order and add the meat last. Cook this at the table in an electric skillet, sukiyaki pan, or a hibachi with a skillet.

Put ½ cup shredded daikon (buy this fresh vegetable at an Oriental market) in each of 6 rice bowls. Melt about 3 tablespoons diced beef fat in heated pan. Add ½ pound sliced fresh mushrooms and cook, stirring, for about 3 minutes. Now add ¼ cup beef consommé and 1 pound spinach leaves (not counting tough stems, which should be discarded), and cook until spinach is wilted. Add 1 pound very thinly sliced beef tenderloin, or eye or rib, or any tender cut. (Ask your meat man to slice it for you on his machine.) Cook, turning with chopsticks, until the meat is done to your liking. Serve over the grated daikon and pass a bottle of soy sauce, the only seasoning. Makes 6 servings.

Hungarian Beef Goulash

There are many different versions of Hungarian goulash (*gulyás*). A favorite is made with sauerkraut. Serve it with noodles, preferably the homemade ones on page 61.

Cut 1 pound lean beef and 1 pound lean pork into 1-inch cubes. Render the fat you have trimmed from the meats. Cook 2 medium-sized sliced onions in ¼ cup of the rendered fat until onions are wilted. Add the meat cubes, and brown on all sides. Add 2 tablespoons paprika, ½ teaspoon marjoram, and 1 pound sauerkraut.

Cover and simmer for 40 minutes, or until meat is tender but not dry and stringy. Salt to taste, then stir in 1 cup sour cream and, if you like the flavor, 1 teaspoon caraway seeds. Makes 6 servings.

Meat and Potato Moussaka

Moussaka, usually thought of as an eggplant dish, is sometimes made with potato in the Middle East. This is a main dish casserole.

- 6 good-sized potatoes, peeled and sliced
- 1 cup minced onion
- ¼ cup butter or salad oil
- 1½ to 2 pounds ground beef or lamb
- 2 tablespoons minced parsley
- 1 can (8 oz.) tomato sauce
- ½ cup water
- Salt and pepper to taste
- 3 cups cream sauce or Béchamel Sauce (page 152)
- Fine dry bread crumbs
- Butter

Parboil potatoes for 6 or 7 minutes; drain. Cook onion in butter until wilted, add ground beef or lamb, and stir over heat for 5 minutes. Add parsley, tomato sauce, water, and salt and pepper. Break up meat and simmer for 15 minutes. Butter a 2½-quart casserole and sprinkle it with crumbs. Arrange the potatoes and meat in layers, pouring some sauce over each layer. Sprinkle top with more crumbs, dot with butter, and bake in a moderate oven (350°) for 30 minutes, or until nicely browned. Makes 6 servings.

Boeuf à la Ficelle

This is "beef on a string." It is rather like a New England boiled dinner, but a very special one that takes two days to cook.

The day before you plan to serve the dinner, make a very rich beef broth: Cover 4 or 5 pounds of beef shank (with some meat on the bones) with 1 gallon of water; add 3 onions, 3 carrots, 3 leeks, 3 small turnips, and 1 large clove garlic, all chopped. Also add an herb bouquet of parsley, bay, thyme, and rosemary; 3 whole cloves, and 1 tablespoon salt. Simmer for 6 hours, replacing water that evaporates. Strain. Chill stock overnight.

In the morning, skim fat from stock. Prepare vegetables: Peel 1 pound small carrots, 12 small boiling onions, and about 6 small turnips. For the meat, purchase a solid, chunky piece of high-grade, well-aged, boneless rump weighing about 4 pounds. Tie it into a compact form with a heavy string (*ficelle*); leave a long, loose piece of string. About 1¼ hours before serving, put the stock in a large pot, add the vegetables, and bring to a boil. Add meat, leaving the loose string hanging out. Cook the meat in the boiling stock exactly 15 minutes for each pound of weight, then pull the meat out by the string. Remove strings, and put meat on a hot platter. Surround with the vegetables. Pour stock into a tureen. Ladle stock over dried French bread or toast in soup bowls. Carve the meat (it will be juicily rare), and serve it and the vegetables along with the soup. Serve a good prepared mustard and a horseradish sauce made by adding 2 tablespoons drained prepared horseradish and ¼ teaspoon salt to 1 cup of sour cream.

Veal Cutlets with Cointreau

A delicious sauce, flavored with Cointreau and lemon juice, makes these veal cutlets special.

Have 6 veal cutlets sliced ½ inch thick. Season with salt and pepper, and brown on both sides in 2 tablespoons butter. Cream together 2 tablespoons butter and 2 tablespoons flour, and let brown slightly, then add 1 cup bouillon and cook until the meat is fork-tender and the sauce thickened. Add the juice of half a lemon, and 2 tablespoons Cointreau. Arrange cutlets on a hot platter, pour on the sauce, and garnish with diamond-shaped pieces of puff or rich pastry. Makes 6 servings.

Veal Balls with Sour Cream

This is a good party dish.

- ½ cup chopped onion
- 1 tablespoon butter
- 1½ pounds lean ground veal (from the shoulder)
- 2 eggs
- ½ cup dry bread crumbs
- 1 cup undiluted evaporated milk
- ¼ cup minced parsley
- 1½ teaspoons salt
- Freshly ground pepper
- ¼ teaspoon crushed rosemary
- ¼ cup shortening
- ¼ cup flour
- ½ cup water or veal stock
- 1½ cups sour cream
- Salt to taste

Sauté onion in butter until wilted. Mix with veal, eggs, bread crumbs, evaporated milk, parsley, salt, a little freshly ground pepper, and rosemary. Form into balls, dust lightly with flour, and brown on all sides in shortening. Remove veal balls to a hot dish. Add flour to the drippings in the pan and mix with the crispings. Pour in water or veal stock, stir until smooth, and then add sour cream. Heat gently (do not boil), season with salt, and pour over the hot meat balls. Makes 6 servings.

Travelers who return from England proudly bearing recipes for the dishes they liked best may be disappointed when they try to cook by them because of the differences in the measuring systems. Dry ingredients are usually weighed, and require a scale. Liquid measures are more of a problem, since several terms mean one thing in England and another here. The English pint, for instance, is 20 ounces (2½ cups)—4 ounces larger than ours. Thus their gill, a measure they use often to indicate ¼ pint, is actually 5 ounces—or, in our terms, ½ cup plus 2 tablespoons. Their "wine glass" measure is half a gill—in our measure, ¼ cup plus 2 tablespoons. Their "teacup" measure is usually 8 ounces, the same as our standard measuring cup.

Saltimbocca

Saltimbocca means "jump-in-mouth" in Italian. It's a good dish, and easy to make. Serve it with spaghetti or noodles, simply dressed with butter and grated Parmesan cheese.

Have 2 ½ pounds of veal cutlets cut thin and in pieces 5 or 6 inches square. Have the same number of thin slices of prosciutto ham cut the same size. Sprinkle the veal with a little ground sage, top with the prosciutto, and fasten together with a wooden pick. Sprinkle with pepper and a little salt, and cook quickly on both sides in 3 tablespoons butter. When the veal is brown, remove to a hot platter (ham side up), and add to the pan ¼ cup water and another 2 tablespoons butter. Stir up the brownings, bring to a boil, and pour over the meat. Makes 6 servings.

French chefs have an impressive method for testing the doneness of meat, though it takes practice. A skewer is thrust deep into the roast, withdrawn, and touched gently to the lips. An experienced chef can tell, from the heat of the skewer, how rare the meat is.

Kalvefilet Oscar

Veal and crab cooked in the Danish manner and served with asparagus is an elegant main dish.

Have ready 24 hot, cooked asparagus tips (fresh, frozen, or canned); in ¼ cup butter lightly sauté 1 pound crab meat in large pieces (preferably legs). Keep warm to serve with the veal.

Have 6 slices cut ¼ inch thick from the top sirloin of veal. Flatten each slice slightly with the flat side of a cleaver or wooden mallet. Dip each slice (both sides) in a mixture of ½ cup flour, 1 teaspoon salt, and a dash of freshly ground pepper. Melt ¼ cup butter in a frying pan and quickly cook the veal in it, turning the meat frequently until brown on both sides.

Remove to a hot platter, divide hot crab meat on top of the cutlets, and arrange the asparagus tips around them. Pour ¼ cup water in the pan in which the meat was cooked; reduce quickly, stirring to incorporate all the brownings; pour over the meat. Serve immediately with Sauce Béarnaise (page 153). Makes 6 servings.

Vitella Tonnato

Here's a French version of that wonderful cold Italian dish, *vitella tonnato.*

Have a 2½-pound piece of veal sliced from the round—this will be a thick veal cutlet. Rub it on both sides with salt, using about 2 tablespoons salt. Roll it up and tie it neatly, then marinate in 1 cup white wine vinegar, 6 chopped green onions, 6 juniper berries (available in spice departments of some food stores), and an herb bouquet of 1 bay leaf, a few sprigs of parsley, and 1 sprig of thyme. Add a chopped carrot and a chopped rib of celery. Marinate in refrigerator for at least 2 full days, preferably 5 or 6, turning each morning and evening.

Remove from marinade, cover with water, and simmer for 1 hour, or until tender. Cool, then spread with a mixture of 1 can anchovies, drained and chopped, 2 tablespoons minced capers, 2 tablespoons minced parsley, and ¼ cup olive oil. Chill, and serve sliced, plain or with mayonnaise, or with a sauce made by whirling together in the blender 1 cup mayonnaise, 1 can (7 oz.) flaked tuna, 2 anchovies, and lemon juice to taste. Makes 6 servings.

Ham and Sour Cream Mousse

Here's a party dish that can be made from bits of leftover ham.

Soak 2 envelopes (2 tablespoons) unflavored gelatin in ¼ cup cold water, then dissolve in ½ cup boiling water. Add 2 cups finely ground cooked ham, ¼ teaspoon dried thyme, and a few grains cayenne. Mix well, then fold in 3 cups sour cream. Taste for seasoning, add salt if needed, and a little mustard, if you wish. Pour into a 5 or 6-cup mold and allow to set. Unmold and serve with a sauce made by combining 1 cup finely chopped and drained cucumber, ¾ cup mayonnaise, 2 tablespoons grated onion, and salt to taste (about ½ teaspoon). Makes 6 to 8 servings.

Noodles with Ham

This is a hearty main dish that needs only a green salad and fresh-baked rolls to complete the menu.

Cut left over ham into pieces the size of a match stick and do the same with fresh mushrooms. You should have approximately 1 cup of each. Sauté together in 3 tablespoons butter. Cook 1 pound noodles until just tender; drain and combine with the ham mixture, 2 tablespoons hot cream, and ½ cup grated Parmesan cheese. Mix gently and serve at once. Makes 6 servings.

Jambon à la Crème

This classic French dish is an elegant way to use slices of leftover cooked ham. You can make it in an electric skillet at the table, if you wish.

For 6 thin slices of ham, cook ¼ cup finely chopped shallots or green onions in ¼ cup butter or margarine until wilted. Stir in ¼ cup flour; cook for 2 minutes, then stir in 1½ cups light cream, ¼ cup white wine or consommé, and 1 tablespoon tomato paste. Correct seasoning. Simmer for 5 minutes, then add the ham slices and allow them to heat. Makes 6 servings.

Ham and Mushroom Toast

A good Sunday night supper dish is made with ham and mushrooms.

Sauté 3 cups sliced mushrooms in 6 tablespoons butter or margarine for 5 minutes. Add 2 tablespoons flour, then stir in ¾ cup bouillon and 1 pint sour cream. Cook, stirring, until smooth; season with salt and pepper and, if you wish, with chives, tarragon, or dill. Put sliced ham on hot buttered toast. Top with the mushrooms, and serve at once. Makes 6 servings.

Stuffed Leg of Lamb

The novice carver will like this lamb roast because he'll have no bones to contend with.

Have your meat man remove all bone from a leg or shoulder of lamb. Lay meat with skin side down, and fill with the mixture below, carefully pushing it into all the cavities. Roll, tie securely in several places, then rub meat with a crushed clove of garlic. Roast in a moderate oven (350°) until the meat thermometer reaches 140° to 145°. (The meat will be pink and juicy; if you like it well done, cook to 165° but no higher, or it will toughen and lose flavor.) Let stand about 15 minutes before slicing. A 5-pound roast will make 8 to 10 servings.

Filling: Mince 1 large onion, and sauté until soft in 2 tablespoons butter or margarine. Add ½ cup quick-cooking cracked wheat or bulghur; cook until lightly browned. Pour in 1 cup stock, made from the lamb bones (or use canned consommé or bouillon). Cover and cook until almost tender (12 to 15 minutes). If necessary, add a little more stock or water. In the meantime, clean and slice 4 to 6 lamb kidneys; sauté in 2 tablespoons butter until the juices stop running. Cool, chop, and mix with the bulghur. Season with a puréed clove of garlic and salt and pepper to taste.

There are two kinds of "pepper steak"—different as East and West. One is the French pepper steak (or steak au poivre) described on page 93, in which coarsely ground black pepper is pressed in liberal amounts into both sides of the raw steak. In the Chinese version of pepper steak, the meat is cut into strips, cooked lightly in oil, and served in a soy-flavored, cornstarch-thickened sauce, with strips of green pepper added—that's where the "pepper" comes in.

Garlic Lamb Patties

These are easy to do, inexpensive, and good.

Have your meat man grind lean shoulder of lamb for you. To each pound, add 1 puréed clove garlic, ¾ teaspoon salt, and some freshly ground pepper. Form into large, fairly thick patties (3 to each pound of meat). Wrap a slice of bacon around the outside of each and broil over charcoal until done to your liking.

Artichoke and Lamb Stew

In Lebanon this is called *yahnit el ardishawki.* Serve it with hot cooked rice.

- 8 medium-sized artichokes
- Water
- Juice of 1 lemon
- 2 pounds boneless lamb, cut in cubes
- ¼ cup flour
- 2 teaspoons salt
- ¼ teaspoon pepper
- ¼ cup salad oil
- 1½ cups chopped onions
- 1 tablespoon flour
- 4 cups water
- 1 teaspoon salt
- Freshly ground pepper
- Additional salt and lemon juice to taste

Wash artichokes; remove stems and coarse outside leaves. Cut off tops about ⅔ of the way down, remove chokes, and cut the remainder into quarters. Cover with water to which you've added the lemon juice. Roll lamb cubes in the ¼ cup flour, seasoned with the 2 teaspoons salt and the ¼ teaspoon pepper.

Heat oil in a Dutch oven or large heavy frying pan; sauté the meat until brown on all sides. Add onions, and when lightly browned, sprinkle with the 1 tablespoon flour; stir until blended. Add water; cover pan and cook for 20 minutes. Add the 1 teaspoon salt, some freshly ground pepper, and the drained artichoke hearts. Cover and cook until tender, about 40 minutes, adding more salt and lemon juice to taste. Makes 8 servings.

Lamb Tarragon

Here's an easy-to-make lamb dish that's interesting enough to serve at a party meal.

Cut 2 pounds lean shoulder of lamb into small pieces and brown with 1 small chopped onion in 2 tablespoons butter or shortening. Stir in 2 tablespoons flour, then add 1½ cups water, ½ cup white wine, 1 teaspoon dried tarragon, 1 teaspoon salt, and a little pepper. Simmer until lamb is tender and the sauce is reduced. Keep over very low heat while blending in ½ cup sour cream. Add salt and pepper, if needed. Serve with hot cooked noodles. Makes about 6 servings.

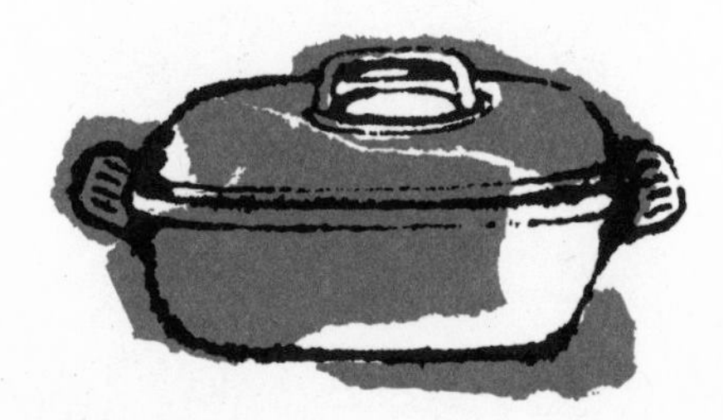

Lamb with Dill Sauce

Lamm med dillsas is the Swedish name for this dish, which is a good choice for a buffet. Tiny boiled potatoes are a good accompaniment.

Select a 4 or 5-pound piece of lamb shoulder and cover with water. Add 2 teaspoons salt, 1 onion, 1 bay leaf, and a few sprigs of dill (or use 2 teaspoons dill weed). Bring to a boil, skim, turn down heat, and simmer for 2 hours, or until the lamb is tender. Strain off stock and reserve. Cut lamb into 1-inch cubes and keep warm. Measure strained stock, and for each cup add 2 teaspoons vinegar, ½ teaspoon sugar, ½ teaspoon dill weed, and salt to taste. Lightly beat egg yolks, using 2 egg yolks for each cup of stock. Heat sauce, and pour 1 cup of it slowly into the beaten egg yolks. Stir this back into remaining sauce, heat but do not boil, and pour over meat. Makes about 6 servings.

Gigot Persille

A *gigot,* or tender leg of baby spring lamb, is one of the great delicacies of France. In our country it is next to impossible to find a lamb leg weighing only 2 or 3 pounds, but those of 5 pounds are not uncommon and are worth looking for.

Cook the leg of lamb in an open roasting pan, in a moderate oven (350°). When it is within about ½ hour of being done to your liking, spread it with a mixture of 1 cup fine dry bread crumbs, ¼ cup melted butter, ¼ cup minced parsley, 1 small clove garlic puréed or crushed with 1 teaspoon salt, and a little pepper. Finish cooking, basting with pan drippings until done the way you like it. In France, lamb is usually served juicily pink—about 140° on a meat thermometer.

Fatiah

This is a sort of pasty, Syrian style, and is a good way to use up the last of a lamb roast. You can freeze it after it's baked to have on hand as an interesting snack. This idea can be used in other ways, too. For instance, substitute cooked beef for lamb and add your own favorite herb or spice. Or wrap well-seasoned raw hamburger patties in the same dough and bake as below, or a little longer if you prefer your meat well done.

- 3 cups ground lamb (including a good portion of fat)
- 1 medium-sized onion, ground
- 1 clove garlic, minced or mashed
- 1 cup pine nuts
- Juice of ½ lemon
- 1 ½ teaspoons salt
- Pepper
- 2 teaspoons ground cinnamon
- Additional salt to taste

- 1 package yeast, active dry or compressed
- ½ cup warm water
- ½ cup milk, scalded, and cooled to lukewarm
- 2 teaspoons sugar
- 1 ½ teaspoons salt
- 1 tablespoon soft butter
- 3 cups sifted flour
- Yogurt or sour cream

Combine meat with onion, garlic, pine nuts, lemon juice, salt, a dash of pepper, and cinnamon. Taste and add more salt, if needed. Set aside. To make yeast dough, dissolve yeast in warm water. Add milk, sugar, salt, and butter. Stir until the butter is melted and blended. Stir in flour. Knead slightly; allow to rise until doubled in bulk.

Turn dough out on a lightly floured board and form into a long roll. Cut into 4 pieces, then cut each of the pieces into 4 pieces, making 16 pieces in all. Roll each piece of dough into a 6-inch circle. Divide the meat mixture into 16 equal portions; put one portion in the center of each dough circle. Pat meat to 3 inches in diameter, then gather up the edges of dough and pinch firmly together in the center. Flatten to a 4-inch circle, turn upside-down on a buttered baking sheet, and allow to rise for 20 minutes. Bake in a moderately hot oven (375°) for about 20 minutes, or until nicely browned. Serve hot with yogurt or sour cream. Makes 8 servings, with 2 pasties per serving.

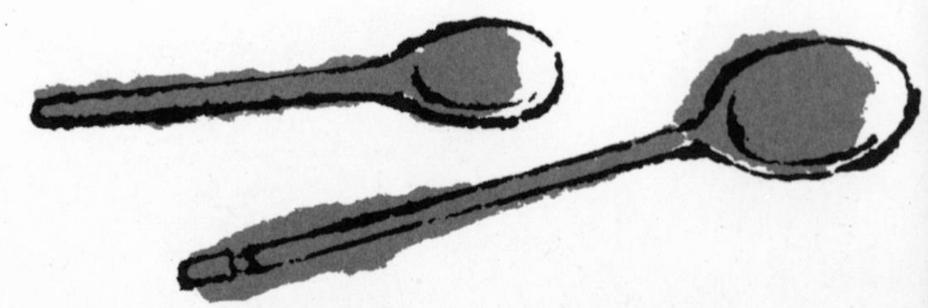

Charcoal-roasted Lamb, Indian Style

Exotic seasonings, typical of India, flavor the stuffing of this lamb roast and permeate the meat as it cooks on the spit.

For the stuffing, combine 3 chopped onions, 3 to 6 minced cloves of garlic, 1 tablespoon ground cumin, 1 chopped green pepper, 2 hot red chili peppers, ½ teaspoon salt, and ¼ teaspoon freshly ground pepper. Pound this to a paste in a mortar, and spread in the center of a boned leg of lamb. Roll the meat securely and tie with string. Put on the spit and roast to the degree you prefer. Baste occasionally with melted butter.

There seems to be some confusion in many cooks' minds as to exactly what it means to "lard" a piece of meat. This confusion has been compounded by many meat cutters who, when asked to lard a roast, merely tie slices of salt pork on it. That is actually "barding." Larding is a process by which long, thin strips of pork fat, or "lardoons," are sewed into the top of the meat with a larding needle. The stitches are usually about an inch long, and both ends of the strips of fat protrude from the top of the meat. The method is particularly useful for meat low in fat content—liver, tenderloin of beef, or a veal roast, or beef round roast, for example.

Lamb Chops, Tarragon

This is a simple but elegant way of serving lamb chops.

Broil 6 thick rib or loin lamb chops until crisply brown on the outside, but pink and juicy within, and serve with the following sauce: Sauté 2 tablespoons minced onion and ½ pound finely chopped fresh mushrooms in 3 tablespoons butter. Cook until the moisture has evaporated; stir in 2 tablespoons flour. Gradually stir in 1 cup white wine in which 2 teaspoons dried tarragon have been soaked (or use 1 tablespoon fresh minced tarragon), and ½ cup heavy cream. Simmer for 10 minutes, correct seasoning, and serve over the broiled lamb chops. Makes 6 servings.

Lamb Chops à la Castellane

There's no reason why the classic sauces and garnishes can't be served with charcoal-grilled meat. These lamb chops are an example.

4 tablespoons butter
3 tablespoons flour
1 cup rich beef stock or beef
  bouillon (undiluted)
¼ cup diced lean ham
3 tablespoons sherry
2 tablespoons minced
  green pepper
6 thick slices unpeeled eggplant
Butter or olive oil
6 thick loin lamb chops
Parsley sprigs or broiled mushroom caps for garnish

Melt 3 tablespoons of the butter. Add flour, and cook, stirring, until lightly browned. Gradually add beef stock or beef bouillon, and cook until smooth and thick. In another pan, cook ham in the remaining 1 tablespoon of butter for a minute or two, then add sherry and green pepper. Add to sauce. When the charcoal fire is good and hot, brush eggplant slices on both sides with butter or olive oil; broil until nicely browned (a hinged broiler makes turning easy). Broil lamb chops as usual, cooking so they are pink and juicy inside, crisply brown outside. Reheat the sauce and pour over the eggplant slices. Put one chop on each slice of eggplant. Garnish with parsley or a broiled mushroom cap, if desired. Makes 6 servings.

Sausage with Grapes

Here's a rather exotic dish to try on your family for breakfast, along with scrambled eggs and plenty of buttered toast.

Buy Italian sweet sausage at an Italian market, allowing 1 pound for 4 to 6 servings. Brown the sausage, add ¼ cup water and 1 cup seeded white grapes to the pan; simmer (covered) for 10 minutes, and serve.

Pork in Milk

This pork is poached rather than roasted. Serve it with mashed potatoes or noodles, a green vegetable, and currant jelly.

Have a 5 or 6-pound piece of pork loin or shoulder boned. Lay it out flat, sprinkle the surface generously with salt and freshly ground pepper, and spread it with 2 puréed garlic cloves. Roll tightly and tie in a compact form. Put in a Dutch oven and add ¼ cup butter or margarine. Brown pork well on all sides, then add milk to cover—2 to 3 quarts. Bring to a boil, then turn down to a simmer. Cover and cook over very low heat for an hour.

Uncover and cook for another hour, or until meat thermometer reads 185° and milk has thickened and lightly browned. (If meat reaches proper temperature before milk is pale brown, remove meat and keep warm and reduce milk by further cooking.)

Remove pork and slice. Arrange on a platter and keep warm. Put browned milk in a blender and whirl until smooth. Season to taste with salt and pepper, reheat, adding a sliced truffle if you feel so inclined, and pour over the pork. Makes 6 to 8 servings.

Schwein Kottlet Budapest

This German pork chop is served with the big fat pimientos that are dearly loved in Hungary.

Have loin pork chops cut about ¾ inch thick. Dip in seasoned flour, then in beaten egg, and finally in fine dry bread crumbs. Cook slowly in a small amount of butter or shortening until tender and brown on both sides, about 1 hour. Remove to a hot platter. In the same pan, heat as many whole canned pimientos as there are chops. Split each hot pimiento and lay on top of a chop.

Slip the platter into a warm oven while you make the gravy: In the frying pan in which the chops were cooked, sauté 1 small chopped onion until brown, adding shortening if needed. Stir in 1 tablespoon flour, ½ cup cream, and 1 cup milk. Cook over medium heat until thickened, about 10 minutes. Season to taste with salt, and pour around the chops on the platter.

Homemade Pork Sausage

Homemade sausage is not difficult to make, and the results are most gratifying.

Grind 3 pounds fresh pork (half fat, half lean), or have your meat man grind it for you. Using your hands, mix it with a small clove of garlic that has been crushed to a paste in 1 tablespoon of salt, 1 finely chopped or ground onion, 1 teaspoon each basil, coarsely ground black pepper, crushed fennel seed, ground coriander, monosodium glutamate, and tarragon, and ¼ teaspoon ground ginger. Form into patties, and fry as usual.

For a different way to cook bacon, sprinkle thick slices lightly with brown sugar. Bake in a moderately hot oven (375° to 400°) until the sugar has melted. Turn bacon, sprinkle with more sugar, and continue baking under the bacon is done to your liking.

Chalupas

These "little boats"—named after the boats in the floating gardens of Xochimilco—are tortillas that hold a green sauce, shredded pork, and chopped onion.

To prepare the pork, cover 1 pound loin with water and cook until very tender. Remove, shred, and return to the stock with ½ teaspoon salt. Simmer until all the water is absorbed.

The sauce is made with green tomatoes. Cut up 3 pounds of green tomatoes and cook in 2 tablespoons lard or butter until soft. Add a sprig of cilantra (you'll find it in Mexican and Chinese stores—it's also called Chinese parsley or fresh coriander), 1 peeled clove of garlic, and 1 peeled green chili. Whirl in a blender or pound in a mortar; add a little salt to taste.

The tortillas are made with fresh masa or with dehydrated masa flour. Make small tortillas (about 4 inches in diameter) according to package directions and cook them on the griddle. While they are hot and soft, turn up the edges like a boat. (Or you can use commercial tortillas and forget the turned-up edges.) Dip them into hot lard or shortening (about 370°) for a minute or so, put on plates, and cover with reheated green sauce and then with shredded cooked pork and chopped onions. Serve at once. Makes enough pork and sauce for 18 small chalupas.

Pork Roast with Beans

Pork and beans, wedded for generations, taste wonderful when combined in this manner. The beans are partially cooked, then finished under a loin of pork. As the meat roasts, it bastes the beans with its rich and savory juices.

Place 1 pound of your favorite dried beans—white, pink, kidney, pinto, or lima–in a large kettle with 8 cups of water; cover, bring to a boil, and cook for 2 minutes. Remove from heat and let soak for 1 hour. Add 2 teaspoons salt, 1 minced clove garlic, and an herb bouquet. Cook for 1 to 2 hours, or until tender (the time will depend on the variety of bean). Drain and reserve liquid, then turn beans into a roasting pan.

Rub salt, pepper, and oregano to taste into a 4 to 6-pound loin of pork. Place meat, fat side up, over the beans. Roast in a 325° oven for 3 to 3½ hours, or until a meat thermometer reads 185°. Stir the beans several times during the cooking, and add some of the reserved liquid if they appear to be drying out. Makes 8 to 10 servings.

Calf's Liver Lyonnaise

This quickly-cooked liver dish goes well with creamed spinach and hash browned potatoes.

Have 2 pounds calf's liver sliced not more than ¼ inch thick. Sprinkle with 1½ teaspoons salt and some freshly ground black pepper, then dredge with ¼ cup flour. Sauté quickly in 3 tablespoons each butter and salad oil. Remove from pan and put on a warm platter in a warm oven. In the same pan sauté 3 large thinly-sliced onions, adding more oil or butter, if necessary. When onions are wilted and slightly brown, put on top of liver. To the pan add 2 teaspoons *glacé de viande* (page 154), 2 tablespoons wine vinegar, and 2 tablespoons water or bouillon, swirling it around to collect all the brownings. Pour over liver and onions and serve at once. Makes 6 servings.

Calf's Liver and Onions, Italian Style

Onions cooked slowly in olive oil complement liver and give Italian flavor to this dish.

Peel and slice 8 large onions, cook slowly, covered, in 3 tablespoons olive oil until completely wilted and a pale amber color. This will take a half hour or longer. Add salt to taste. Slice 1 ½ pounds tender calf's liver as thinly as possible. Sprinkle with salt and pepper, and put on top of the hot onions. Turn up heat and cook very quickly for about 2 minutes; the liver should then be done. Serve at once. Makes 6 to 8 servings.

Tarragon Liver

To make liver a delicacy, have it cut an inch thick, and sauté it quickly in butter. When it's brown outside but still pink inside, remove it to a hot platter. For each pound of liver, put into same pan in which liver was cooked 1 mashed clove garlic, 3 tablespoons butter, and 2 teaspoons tarragon vinegar. Cook this mixture until the garlic is soft, mashing it again. Strain over the liver, and sprinkle with minced parsley and tarragon.

Langue de Boeuf à la Vinaigrette

In France, the muzzle of beef *(museau de boeuf)* is a delicacy, but it is not generally obtainable here. Fresh beef tongue is fairly similar in flavor to beef muzzle, and makes a reasonable facsimile when boiled as usual, skinned, sliced paper-thin, and served with a French dressing to which minced parsley, green onions, and olives are added. Serve it cold as a first course, or as one of the dishes on a party buffet.

Kidneys Flambé

Too much cooking toughens kidneys; they should be slightly pinkish to be at their best. Here's an easy, classic way to prepare them.

Skin and trim 1 veal kidney or 4 lamb kidneys. Cook quickly in ¼ cup hot melted butter until lightly browned. (This should not take more than 2 minutes for the lamb kidneys, 4 for the veal.) Cut in slices—they will be quite red inside—and return to the pan. Add a jigger of brandy and light it.

When the flames die down, add ½ cup white wine, 1 teaspoon prepared mustard, 2 tablespoons minced chives, 2 tablespoons minced parsley, some salt, and a dash of cayenne. Cook for another 3 or 4 minutes, shaking the pan. Remove from heat and add a small piece of butter; as soon as butter melts, pour kidneys into a hot dish and serve with triangles of toast. Makes 3 servings.

Kidneys in Tarragon Cream

Exciting flavor harmony results when kidneys are served in this creamy tarragon-flavored sauce.

- 1½ pounds kidneys (about 10 lamb kidneys or 2 veal kidneys)
- ¼ cup butter
- 4 minced shallots or green onions
- 2 teaspoons tarragon
- 1½ cups heavy cream
- Salt and pepper to taste
- 1 tablespoon brandy, sherry, or Madeira (optional)
- Pastry or toast triangles for garnish

Slice kidneys, discarding skin and tough part of tubes. Heat butter in a heavy frying pan; add shallots or green onions and the kidneys. Cook quickly, turning to sear all sides. When the kidneys have lost their raw look, but are still pink, add tarragon and cream. Sprinkle with salt and pepper; raise the heat to reduce the cream by one third. (If kidneys start to lose their pink look, remove them from the pan and keep warm until the sauce is reduced and thickened.) Add the brandy, sherry, or Madeira, if used. Pour sauce over kidneys and garnish with triangles of pastry or toast. Makes 6 servings.

Braised Oxtails

As *queue de boeuf, braisée,* this humble dish has starred at many a Frenchman's table. Served with crusty bread or boiled potatoes and a fruit dessert, it makes a distinguished yet economical meal.

12 small whole onions
¼ pound bacon, diced
2 disjointed oxtails
¼ cup flour
1 teaspoon salt
½ teaspoon pepper
1 clove garlic, puréed
6 small carrots, scraped
2 cups white wine
1 can (1 lb.) tomatoes
Herb bouquet (parsley, bay, thyme)
Water
2 tablespoons flour
1 cup water
Minced parsley

Peel onions and cook with bacon until lightly browned. Remove onions and bacon from pan. Dust oxtails in the ¼ cup flour, sprinkle with salt and pepper, and brown in bacon fat in the pan. Add garlic, return onions to pan, add carrots, white wine, tomatoes, herb bouquet, and enough water just to cover. Cover and cook very slowly for 2½ hours, or until fork-tender. Skim off fat (a good way is to refrigerate it overnight and then lift off the hardened fat). To the sauce add the 2 tablespoons flour mixed with the 1 cup water. Cook until thickened. Correct seasoning and serve sprinkled with minced parsley. Makes 6 servings.

Sulz

If you like pigs' feet, try this delicious cold meat loaf.

Have 8 front feet split in half. Cover with cold water, add 1 tablespoon salt, 3 bay leaves, 1 sliced onion, 8 peppercorns, and 1 small dried hot red chili. Bring to a boil, skim, and simmer on low heat until the feet are very, very tender—about 3 hours. Remove pigs' feet and reduce liquid by rapid boiling until you have 2 cups broth; add ⅔ cup cider vinegar.

Remove meat from bones in fairly good-sized pieces. Pack into a small loaf pan (about 4 by 8 inches). Taste reduced broth and add more salt or vinegar if needed; it should be robust in flavor. Pour broth over meat and refrigerate until firmly set. Turn out of the pan, and serve in slices as you would head cheese, or in cubes on picks as an appetizer.

Tongue Mousse

Tongue Mousse is a delicious cold meat dish to serve at a buffet.

Cover a smoked tongue with cold water, bring to a boil. (If this water tastes quite salty, drain, and again cover meat with water and bring to a boil.) Simmer for 3 or 4 hours, or until tender. Remove skin and bones, and grind the meat.

For each 2 cups of ground meat, soak 1 envelope unflavored gelatin in ¼ cup cold water. Add ¾ cup boiling beef bouillon, stir until dissolved, and chill until partially set. Add to the meat, along with ¼ cup mayonnaise, 1 teaspoon prepared mustard, 2 tablespoons grated onion, 1 tablespoon minced parsley, 1 tablespoon lemon juice, ¼ teaspoon dill weed, and ¼ cup cream, whipped. Add salt, if needed, and a dash of cayenne.

Pour into a mold—size depending upon the number of cups of tongue (2 cups, a 4-cup mold; 4 cups, a 6-cup mold; 6 cups, a 2-quart mold). Allow to set, unmold on a bed of shredded lettuce, and serve with a sauce made by combining 1 cup each sour cream and mayonnaise with 2 tablespoons drained prepared horseradish.

Lamb Tongues, Vinaigrette

Lamb tongues, when you can find them, are inexpensive. Served cold, this is an excellent addition to a buffet.

Allow 1 or 2 tongues per person, depending upon the size of the complete meal. Cover with court bouillon (or canned bouillon diluted with water and seasoned with an herb bouquet of parsley, celery leaves, an onion stuck with cloves, and a bay leaf) and simmer until tender (1 to 1½ hours). Drain and peel the tongues, split lengthwise, and arrange attractively in a shallow serving dish.

Make a vinaigrette sauce with ½ cup olive oil (part can be salad oil), 3 tablespoons wine vinegar, 1 teaspoon salt, a dash of freshly ground pepper, 1 teaspoon minced chives, 1 teaspoon minced parsley, ½ teaspoon minced tarragon, and a half of a hard-cooked egg. (This will be enough sauce for 2 pounds of tongues.) Pour over the meat and refrigerate for 24 hours. Turn several times, to keep the meat coated with the sauce.

Civet of Hare

A *civet,* as perhaps you know, is a ragout made of furred game and red wine. Originally the sauce was thickened with the blood of the animal, but since this is impossible when you buy your game from the meat market, even culinary purists will sanction the omission. This dish has a kind of humble elegance that makes it worthy of appearance at guest meals. Serve it with red wine and a good crusty bread.

Have a large rabbit (about 2½ pounds) cut into pieces for serving. Reserve the liver. In a Dutch oven, melt ¼ cup butter. Add 4 slices bacon, cut in dice, arrange the hare on top, and cook gently for 15 minutes, turning once. Add 1 cup chopped green onions and 1 pressed clove garlic, and cook for a few minutes more. Sprinkle with ¼ cup flour, turning the meat as you do, so that all will be coated.

Cook for 3 or 4 minutes, then add an herb bouquet of parsley, bay leaf, and thyme, and 3 cups red wine. Season with salt and pepper and bring to a rapid boil. Cook until the sauce thickens, then add ½ pound sliced mushrooms. Cover and simmer for 1½ to 2 hours, or until the meat is tender but not stringy.

Chop the raw liver, making sure to catch all the juice. Put in a saucepan with a jigger of cognac (3 tablespoons), and bring to a boil. Cook for 2 minutes, then add to the sauce in the pot. Mix well and serve. Makes about 4 servings.

Tripe Casserole

Tripe is becoming more and more popular. Here's a recipe for it that will appeal to epicures.

Cook 2 pounds tripe in salted water to cover until tender, about 1 hour. Drain and cut in strips about 1 by 2 inches. Chop 1 large onion and cook it in 2 tablespoons butter until wilted; add 1 can (10¾ oz.) brown gravy, 1 finely minced clove garlic, 2 cans (8 oz. each) tomato sauce, and the cooked tripe; simmer until the sauce is thick (about 15 minutes). Mix in ¼ cup minced parsley, ½ teaspoon oregano, and 1 tablespoon lemon juice. Put in a casserole, sprinkle with about ¼ cup grated Parmesan cheese, and brown under the broiler.

Poultry

Gone are the days when chicken was considered a Sunday dinner treat and turkey was reserved for those important Thanksgiving and Christmas feasts. Today poultry is plentiful and economical and a favorite of most cooks. It is a wonderfully versatile food that appeals to almost everyone and that can be prepared in many different ways. Its delicate taste stands admirably on its own, yet marries harmoniously with many other flavors—even those as strong as curry. Even its leftovers can be glamorized.

Cooks from almost every country of the world prize poultry, lavish loving care upon it, and serve it with pride. Some of the most famous dishes of *haute cuisine* feature chicken in one form or another—yet this wonderful bird is just as much at home at a barbecue. Turkeys, too, and ducks and squabs, are equally versatile, and give enthusiastic cooks a great opportunity to try new and fascinating recipes.

There are recipes for many types of poultry dishes here. They're sure to win praise, and to become favorites that you'll want to repeat often—either as they are here, or with your own individual touches.

Chicken San Marino

This dish using only the breast of chicken is an elegant one for a party meal. Accompany it with a green vegetable such as peas, and with potato balls.

Allow 2 breast pieces (the entire breast of 1 chicken, split) for each guest. For each breast piece, wrap a ¼-inch slice of Gruyère or Emmenthal cheese (about 1 by 2½ inches) in a very thin piece of prosciutto or Virginia ham. Put boned breasts between two pieces of waxed paper and pound them with the flat side of a cleaver or heavy knife. Wrap each chicken breast piece securely around a ham packet, covering it completely. Dust with seasoned flour, then dip in slightly beaten egg. Let dry for a half hour or so, then again dip in beaten egg and roll in fine bread crumbs. These may now be refrigerated.

Brown breasts carefully on both sides in melted butter, then arrange on a heat-proof platter and finish cooking in a moderate oven (350°) for about 10 minutes, or until fork-tender. Don't allow them to dry out. Into the pan in which they were browned put 1 jigger (3 tablespoons) cognac for each 8 breast pieces; flame, and when the flame dies down add ½ cup heavy cream. Simmer until thickened; add salt and pepper to taste. Pour sauce over the chicken just before serving.

Sesame Chicken

Sesame seed flavors the crisp brown crust of this chicken.

Have 1 broiler-fryer cut in pieces. Combine 1 slightly beaten egg and ½ cup milk. In another small bowl, mix together ½ cup flour, ¼ cup sesame seed, 1 teaspoon salt, and ¼ teaspoon freshly ground pepper. Melt ¼ cup butter in a baking pan. Dip chicken parts in milk mixture, then in flour. Put chicken in pan, turning so that butter coats all sides. Bake in a moderate oven (350°) for 1 to 1¼ hours, or until tender, brown, and crisp. Makes about 4 servings.

Onion-Stuffed Chicken

This recipe comes from Brittany, and it is as easy as it is sensational.

Peel 1½ pounds small white onions and put them in a heavy pan with 2 tablespoons butter and 1 tablespoon water. Cover and cook for 15 minutes, shaking the pan occasionally. Sprinkle with salt and pepper, put into the cavity of a roasting chicken, close, truss, and roast as usual.

Have you ever been stumped by what wine to serve with Chinese food? The Chinese rice wines are not always appreciated here, and neither hot sake, as served with Japanese food, nor champagne is a perfect answer. Recently a new wine called Quang-jo has made its appearance in Chinese restaurants. It's simply sauterne, heated with a piece of peeled fresh ginger—one small nubbin (about 1 inch) for each bottle. The ginger flavor should be very subtle, so don't let it stand; bring wine to the simmering point, remove ginger, and cool.

Chicken Scallopini

If you have difficulty in getting young white veal for scallopini, try using chicken breasts. They are less expensive than most veal. The pounded-out chicken will cook in 2 to 4 minutes, and will be wonderfully moist, tender, and flavorful. This is a good dish to cook at the table, in an electric frying pan. For an even simpler dish, omit the breading.

For each 2 servings, allow 2 breast pieces (breast of 1 chicken, split). Remove bones from chicken pieces. Put each breast piece between 2 pieces of waxed paper and pound thin with a rolling pin or mallet until about twice its original size, taking care not to tear the meat. Dip each in seasoned flour (½ cup flour, 1 teaspoon salt, dash of pepper), shake off surplus, dip into 1 egg slightly beaten with 1 tablespoon of milk, then roll in fine dry bread crumbs. At this point the breasts may be refrigerated until needed. Just before serving, sauté the breasts in butter, cooking quickly until brown on one side, then turning and browning on the other. Serve with wedges of lemon.

Chicken en Coquilles

Adventurous cooks are pleased when there are pieces of chicken left from a meal, for they can reappear in most glamorous guises, as in this luncheon dish. Leftover turkey or veal can be used this way, too.

Mix 2 cups of chopped, cooked chicken with 1 cup Béchamel Sauce (page 152) or a mushroom sauce; season either sauce to your taste. (You'll need another ½ cup of the sauce later.) Cook 2 bunches of well washed spinach in a minimum of water until wilted; drain, pressing out any remaining moisture. Chop spinach and mix with 2 tablespoons butter, and salt and pepper to taste. Divide among 6 scallop shells or individual ramekins. Cover with the meat mixture, then spread the remaining ½ cup of sauce over the tops. Top with a large sautéed mushroom cap, if you wish, or sprinkle with crumbs or grated cheese or nuts. Heat in a moderate oven (350°) for 20 minutes. Makes 6 servings.

Alsatian Chicken

This chicken is lightly browned, then simmered in a sauce richly flavored with mushrooms and wine.

- 2 broiler-fryers, cut into serving-size pieces
- ¼ cup butter
- 6 chopped shallots or green onions
- ½ pound mushrooms, sliced
- 1 teaspoon salt
- Freshly ground pepper
- 1 cup Riesling or Traminer wine
- Herb bouquet (parsley, bay, and thyme)
- 2 egg yolks
- ½ cup light cream

Brown chicken lightly in butter. Add shallots or green onions and mushrooms. Sprinkle with salt and pepper. Cook for 4 or 5 minutes, then add wine and herb bouquet; cover and simmer for 30 minutes, or until the meat is tender. Put chicken on a platter and keep warm.

Remove herb bouquet and reduce sauce by half. Beat egg yolks with cream, and add a little of the hot mixture, whisking constantly. Add cream mixture to the remaining broth and cook over low heat for a minute or two, or until slightly thickened. Stir constantly and do not allow sauce to boil. Correct seasoning and pour over the chicken. Makes 6 to 8 servings.

Chicken Marengo

The story (perhaps apocryphal) of how Napoleon's chef created Chicken Marengo from the pickups of a war-ravaged farm in Piedmont is well known among food historians. But it doesn't account for the later refinements of this classic dish—the garnishes of fried egg, truffles, and heart-shaped croûtons. But no matter—the recipe is as good now as when it was first born.

1 broiler-fryer, cut in serving-size pieces
Salt and pepper
¼ cup olive oil or salad oil
½ cup white wine
1 small clove garlic, finely minced
10 small whole mushrooms
2 tomatoes, peeled, seeded, and chopped (or ¼ cup tomato purée)
1 truffle, sliced (optional)
4 slices bread
4 small eggs
Minced parsley

Sprinkle chicken with salt and pepper, and sauté in oil, turning to brown evenly. Remove chicken pieces to a shallow baking dish (about 2-quart size). To the pan add wine, garlic, mushrooms, tomatoes, and the sliced truffle, if used. Let cook for 6 minutes, adding a little water or chicken stock if sauce becomes too thick. Taste sauce and add salt if necessary. Pour over the chicken, cover, and bake in a moderate oven (350°) for half an hour, or until the chicken is tender. (Or instead of baking this dish, return the chicken to the sauté pan, cover, and cook slowly until tender.)

For the garnish, cut each bread slice into a heart shape and toast on both sides. (The French fry them in butter.) Fry eggs in a small amount of butter; trim with a round cutter. To serve, arrange chicken on a platter, pour over the sauce, sprinkle with minced parsley, and arrange the garnishes around the edge of the platter. (For a plainer version of this dish, you can skip the garnishes.) Makes 4 servings.

Chicken in Vermouth

With all the cooking that is done with wine and herbs, it is surprising that vermouth isn't used more often in the kitchen. After all, it is a combination of wine and herbs. Try this simple recipe and you'll be cooking with this apéritif wine more often.

Have broiler-fryer chickens cut in quarters, allowing 1 chicken for each 2 or 3 persons. For each 2 to 2½-pound chicken, melt 3 tablespoons butter with a slice of garlic. Remove garlic and brush chicken with mixture. Put in a baking pan, skin side up, and bake in a moderately hot oven (375°) for 30 minutes. For each chicken, add ¼ cup dry vermouth to the pan, and baste chicken with mixture. Continue cooking for 30 minutes, or until the chicken is fork-tender and brown, basting with the vermouth and juices in the pan.

If you've ever puzzled over the exact meaning of "entrée," you may be comforted to know that even the French have no absolute definition. In France it is usually the course that follows the fish. In elaborate menus, however, it may be the third course, for a relevé, or "remove," often comes after the fish and before the entrée. And a recent cook book, translated from the French, claims that the entrée is the first course, and thus may be soup or appetizer or fish course. Here in our country, entrée has come to mean the main course.

Nasi Goreng

This is an Indonesian favorite. It's an adaptable dish; you can use any left-over meat, or you can add fish or shellfish, fresh, frozen, or canned.

1 pound white rice
1 bunch green onions
2 tablespoons salad oil
1 pound shredded cooked chicken, turkey, or veal
½ pound shredded cooked ham
1 small pressed clove garlic

Cook rice until tender but dry. Chop onions, including tender part of stems. Sauté onions in oil for 2 minutes. Add chicken, ham, and garlic. Combine with rice, and fry all together, adding extra oil as needed. Makes 8 servings.

Garlic Chicken

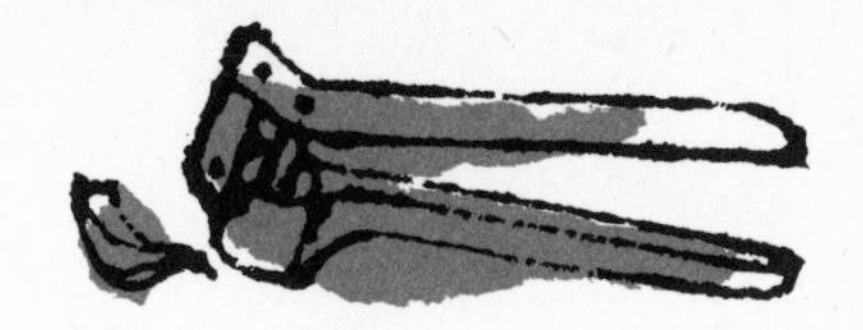

Those who enjoy robust garlic flavor will like this Garlic Chicken. Lemon juice adds a tangy complement to the garlic.

- 2½ to 3-pound broiler-fryer, cut in serving-size pieces
- ¼ cup butter or margarine
- 2 tablespoons olive oil or salad oil
- 2 teaspoons salt
- Freshly ground pepper
- 1 clove garlic, mashed or finely minced
- ¼ cup minced green onions
- 2 tablespoons lemon juice
- ½ teaspoon minced fresh or crushed dried marjoram
- ¼ cup white wine

In a large frying pan that has a lid, brown chicken on all sides in butter and olive oil. Mix together salt, pepper, garlic, green onions, lemon juice, and marjoram. Pour over chicken, cover, and simmer on top of the range for 30 minutes, or until fork-tender. Remove chicken to a warm platter, add wine to the pan, and heat, scraping up the brownings left in the bottom of the pan. Pour over the chicken. Makes 4 servings.

Chicken Valle d'Auge

Apple brandy, used to flame this chicken, adds delicate overtones of flavor. For an elegant accompaniment, serve artichoke bottoms piled high with a purée of cooked and seasoned peas. Serve rice, if you wish, but it's not necessary.

Have 2 broiler-fryers cut in serving-size pieces; wash and dry thoroughly and brown on all sides in ¼ cup butter. Cover and cook slowly until just tender, not more than 30 minutes. Sprinkle with salt and pepper. Heat ½ cup Calvados (apple brandy) or applejack, and pour over the chicken. Light and baste chicken with the flaming liquor. When the fire dies down, remove chicken to a hot platter and keep warm.

Lightly beat 4 egg yolks, add 1 cup light cream, and pour into the pan in which the chicken cooked. Stir constantly over very low heat until the sauce thickens. Do not let it boil. Correct seasoning and strain over the chicken. Makes 6 servings.

Polla all' Diavolo

This is broiled chicken in the Florentine manner. Try it on your charcoal grill. Serve with spaghetti dressed with butter and grated Parmesan cheese, and with green beans mixed with crisp, diced salt pork and plenty of minced chives.

Have broiler-fryer chickens split down the back and opened out flat—this is called a "spatchcock." Brush chickens liberally with olive oil. For each chicken mix together 1 pressed clove garlic and 1 teaspoon ground ginger. Rub this all over the bird, then sprinkle with finely minced parsley. Broil over charcoal, cut side down first, then turn and brown the other side. This will take 25 to 45 minutes, depending upon the fire and the size and temperature of the bird.

Chicken Litchi

Here's an exotic chicken dish using canned litchi nuts.

3-pound broiler-fryer, cut in pieces
½ cup flour
1 teaspoon each salt and powdered ginger
½ teaspoon thyme
½ cup (¼ pound) butter or margarine
1½ cups dry white wine
1 can (16 oz.) litchi nuts

Dust chicken with a mixture of the flour, salt, ginger, and thyme. Melt butter and brown chicken in it, adding more butter if necessary. Remove to a casserole. Pour wine into frying pan, stir with drippings, and pour over chicken. Cover and bake in a moderate oven (350°) until chicken is tender, about 30 minutes. Drain litchi nuts and add. Return to the oven until the litchis are hot, about 10 minutes. Makes 4 servings.

Chicken Kiev

This famous dish is not at all difficult to make, and it makes an elegant dinner entrée. In restaurants, part of the wing is usually left on the chicken and decorated with a frill. We've omitted this, because most cooks buy chicken breasts separately, without the wings.

6 pieces chicken breast (breasts of 3 chickens, split)
⅓ cup butter
1 small clove garlic, pressed
1 teaspoon minced parsley
½ teaspoon minced or crumbled marjoram
2 tablespoons flour
1 large egg, beaten
¾ cup fine dry bread crumbs
Watercress for garnish
Drawn Butter Sauce (below)

Remove skin and bones from chicken breasts, being careful not to cut into the meat. You'll notice that each piece has one large and one smaller fillet; in each of these there is a silvery cord. Pressing the meat down firmly on the table with one hand, pull out these tendons with pliers. Put chicken breasts between two pieces of heavy waxed paper and pound gently and evenly until the pieces flatten to twice their original width.

Cream butter with garlic, parsley, and marjoram. Form into 6 fingers about 2 inches long; chill well (a short sojourn in the freezer will hasten the job). Put a finger of butter on the most ragged end of each chicken breast and roll, tucking the edges in as you go. The butter should be completely enclosed. Dust rolls with flour. Roll chicken in egg, covering completely, and then in bread crumbs. There should be no holes in the coating. Chill, then fry in deep fat at 350° until nicely browned. Serve garnished with watercress and Drawn Butter Sauce. Makes 6 servings.

Drawn Butter Sauce: Melt 3 tablespoons butter, add 3 tablespoons flour, and cook for 1 minute, stirring. Add 1½ cups chicken stock, stir smooth, and simmer for 10 minutes. Add ½ teaspoon lemon juice, salt and pepper to taste, and 3 more tablespoons butter. Serve as soon as butter is melted.

Chicken Sauté

Green ripe olives are a delicious addition to a simple dish such as this.

Have two 2-pound broiler-fryers disjointed. Cook them quickly in ¼ cup hot olive oil or salad oil in a heavy pan (brown lightly on all sides). Add 1 can (1 lb.) tomatoes, 1 large puréed clove garlic, ¼ cup minced parsley, ½ teaspoon basil, salt and pepper to taste, and 1 cup white table wine. Cover and simmer for 20 minutes, then add 1 cup green ripe olives (cut from their pits before measuring). Cook for another 10 minutes or until the sauce is reduced one-half. Serve with hot rice. Makes about 6 servings.

Fricasseed Chicken

How long has it been since you've served good old-fashioned fricasseed chicken? Broiler-fryers and roasters have become so plentiful and consequently so inexpensive that many of us forget our mothers' old stand-by, the stewing hen. For the real essence of chicken flavor, this is it.

Have the chicken disjointed and dust it with flour, then brown it lightly in some of the excess fat that an old hen always has, using the pot in which you intend to stew it. Add water—just enough to come to the top of the chicken—and an onion, half a bay leaf, a little thyme or rosemary, and salt. Cover and simmer until tender to the fork, the length of time depending on the age of the chicken. Don't overcook, or the meat will be dry. Skim off fat and thicken the gravy with a roux of flour and the fat or butter, allowing 2 tablespoons each for each cup of gravy. Serve in a deep dish, sprinkle with minced parsley, and pass extra gravy—with rice, noodles, dumplings, mashed potatoes, or hot biscuits.

Chicken Livers in Cream

This is an excellent choice for a party brunch.

Cut 1 pound chicken livers in halves and sauté in ¼ cup butter, along with 1 tablespoon minced shallots or green onions. When lightly browned, sprinkle with salt and pepper, and pour a jigger of cognac over them. Light and allow the flames to die out (this burns away the alcohol, leaving only the flavor). Now add 1 cup heavy cream and cook quickly until cream is reduced about one-third. Sprinkle with some very finely minced parsley, and serve on toast, or with Sesame French Toast (page 160). Makes 4 to 6 servings.

Chicken Livers with Rice Ring

Fill a rice ring with these chicken livers and serve for lunch. Or serve on toast, or with scrambled eggs or an omelet for breakfast or brunch.

- 1 pound mushrooms, sliced
- 5 tablespoons butter
- 8 bacon slices
- 2 chopped shallots or green onions
- 1 pound chicken livers, cut in half
- Salt and pepper
- 2 tablespoons flour
- ½ cup chicken stock
- ¾ cup mellow sherry
- 1 tablespoon wine vinegar

Sauté mushrooms in 3 tablespoons of the butter; reserve. In another pan cook bacon until crisp; remove and drain on paper towels. Pour off all but 1 tablespoon of the drippings, add the remaining 2 tablespoons of butter and the shallots or green onions. Sauté until the onions are soft, then add chicken livers. Sprinkle with salt and pepper and brown on all sides. Remove and reserve with the mushrooms. To the pan add flour and stir smooth. Then gradually stir in chicken stock, sherry, and wine vinegar. Stir until all the brown particles are incorporated in the sauce and the sauce thickens. If the sauce becomes too thick, add a little more chicken stock. When hot and smooth, add the mushrooms, chicken livers, and crumbled bacon and heat quickly. Makes 6 servings.

Chicken Livers in Madeira

Serve this quick chicken liver sauce on toast or in a rice ring for luncheon, with a simple salad.

Melt ¼ cup butter in a frying pan. Cut 1 pound chicken livers in halves, and add to pan. Cook gently, turning occasionally, until the pink juices have just disappeared. Sprinkle the livers with salt and pepper, and put into a very slow oven to keep warm while making the sauce.

To the pan in which the livers were cooked, add 2 tablespoons flour and stir over low heat until smooth. Gradually add ½ cup chicken stock and cook for 3 or 4 minutes to remove the raw taste of the flour, then add ½ cup Madeira wine. As soon as sauce bubbles, add ½ cup sour cream and stir until smooth. (Do not allow to boil.) Taste for seasoning, adding salt if necessary. Pour over the livers and serve at once. Makes about 4 servings.

Gizzards en Brochette

Chicken gizzards are a wonderful buy and may be served in many delicious ways. You can do them this way in the kitchen or, for an outdoor meal, over the charcoal grill. The gizzards may also be wrapped in quarter-slices of bacon, fastened with toothpicks, and broiled for an interesting appetizer.

Barely cover 3 pounds cleaned chicken gizzards, 2 sliced onions, and an herb bouquet (parsley, bay, and thyme) with salted water, and simmer until tender—about 1 hour. Drain (but save that wonderful stock). Cool and trim off any tough parts, and cut in halves. Put a skewer through one end of a slice of bacon, string gizzards on the skewer, then wind the bacon around them, spearing the other end with the skewer. Broil or grill over charcoal, turning to crisp on all sides. Makes 6 generous servings.

Curried Chicken Gizzards

Chicken gizzards are inexpensive and remarkably rich in flavor. Try them curried, for a party meal. Serve them with rice, and accompany with chutney, chopped green onions, crisp bits of bacon, grated apple and coconut mixed together with a little lemon juice, chopped peanuts, and sliced bananas.

3 pounds chicken gizzards
2 quarts cold water
1 onion, cut up
Herb bouquet
1 teaspoon salt
2 cloves garlic, crushed
¼ cup butter
1 tablespoon curry powder
½ cup flour
Salt and pepper to taste
1 cup yogurt

Clean gizzards, cover with the cold water; add onion, herb bouquet, and salt, and simmer until tender, about 2 hours. Strain and reduce stock to 1 quart; cut gizzards into pieces. Cook garlic in butter for 2 minutes. Discard garlic, add gizzards and curry powder. Blend in flour, and gradually add the 1 quart reduced stock. Add salt and pepper to taste (and more curry, if you wish). Cook until thickened and the raw flour taste has disappeared. Add yogurt, reheat, and serve with accompaniments suggested above. Makes 8 to 10 servings.

Charcoal-grilled Cornish Game Hens

Cornish game hens are as at home on the patio as they are on a formal dinner table. They are actually at their best when eaten in the fingers so that not a tender morsel is lost. Squab pigeons can be cooked in this manner, too. Allow 1 Cornish game hen or squab for each person.

Split the birds down the backs and flatten them, then brush with olive oil or salad oil (or equal parts oil and dry vermouth). Broil, first with the skin side up, over a good bed of glowing coals. Turn and baste occasionally while broiling. Broil for 25 to 35 minutes, or until juices run clear when bird is pierced with a skewer.

Sautéed Squabs

Although "squab" can broadly designate such young birds as a nestling chicken, a pheasant, or even a turkey, the term is generally used to mean a squab pigeon. Young pigeons, or *pigeonneaux*, are usually at their best when they're about four weeks old and weigh about a pound. They are generally available, but you'll probably have to place a special order with your meat man. Here's a delicious, simply way to prepare them.

Have squabs split down the middle and cook, skin side down, in butter. When brown, sprinkle with salt and pepper, turn, put cover on pan, and cook for another 20 minutes, or until the legs feel tender or the juice runs clear. Remove birds to a warm platter and add a few tablespoons of white wine to the pan. Simmer for 4 or 5 minutes, scraping up all the little brown bits from the bottom of the pan, then serve over the squabs.

Charcoal-roasted Duck

Roast duck, cooked on a spit over charcoal, makes a nice change from chicken or roast turkey. You can stuff it if you wish, but it's not necessary.

Because a duck is so compact, it doesn't have to be trussed. Spit it and roast without basting for about 1¼ hours (or longer, if necessary to crisp the skin). Be sure to catch the drippings in a pan under and in front of the spit. Serve with Sauce Rouennaise. A good-sized duck will serve 3 or 4.

Sauce Rouennaise: Dice a medium-sized onion; cook in 1 tablespoon butter until soft and just beginning to color. Add ½ cup red wine, ¼ cup of the drippings from the duck, and 1 can (10½ oz.) beef bouillon that has been simmered until reduced to ¼ cup. Add a few drops of lemon juice and salt and pepper to taste. Strain before serving.

Chicken or Turkey Stuffing

An unusual stuffing for roast chicken or turkey (it can also be used for Cornish game hen or squab) comes from North Africa.

Combine 6 cups cooked rice, ¾ cup seedless raisins that have been plumped in boiling water, ¾ cup toasted chopped almonds, ⅛ teaspoon powdered saffron dissolved in 1 teaspoon hot water, ½ teaspoon ground cinnamon, ¼ cup salad oil or melted butter, and salt and pepper to taste. Mix all together lightly. This is enough for 2 roasting chickens. Double the recipe for a 16 to 18-pound turkey.

Papillote, in French, means curl paper, the kind used by French women before the days of the permanent. It also has a culinary meaning, known to gastronomes everywhere. It is method of cooking in which fish, meat, or fowl is wrapped and cooked in paper. It is said that this was started by Madame de Maintenon who, in order to pamper her ailing royal spouse's stomach, cooked his mutton chops in curl papers to preserve their salubrious juices. Chefs everywhere adopted the trick. The food to be cooked was laid on one side of a large heart-shaped piece of paper, seasonings and sauces were added, and the paper was folded and sealed to form a "half-heart" packet. The food was cooked and served in the paper, so that when the diner opened it, he was greeted by all the nice aroma that had been captured and held. Moderns still use this form of cooking, though many of them substitute foil for the paper; it is easier to seal.

Turkey Marco Polo

This is a popular dish that seems to be turning up in several guises. This version, a very good one, comes from one of California's finest restaurants.

Cook 2 pounds fresh broccoli until tender-crisp. Drain and arrange it on a heat-proof platter or baking dish. Cover with ¼ pound thinly-sliced ham or prosciutto, then with ¾ to 1 pound sliced cooked breast of turkey. Cover with 3 cups Sauce Mornay (page 152), and sprinkle with ¼ cup grated Parmesan cheese. Bake in a moderate oven (350°) until the sauce is hot and the cheese brown and bubbly, about 15 minutes. Makes 6 servings.

Turkey Encore

This is an excellent way to use up leftover cooked turkey.

Cut a sandwich loaf in slices 2 inches thick. Trim off crusts; about 3/8 inch in from the edge of each slice, make a cut 1 1/2 inches deep all around the perimeter, following the shape of the bread. Brush with melted butter and bake in a hot oven (400°) for 15 minutes, or until brown. Scoop out center section.

Dice turkey meat fine, and add 3 cups of it to 2 cups of this Velouté Sauce: Cook 3 tablespoons butter or turkey fat with 3 1/2 tablespoons flour; add 1 cup rich turkey stock, made from the carcass, and 1 cup cream. Cook until smooth and thick, and season to taste with salt and pepper and a very little nutmeg. Put the bread cases on individual plates and half fill with the turkey mixture. Top with a poached egg that has been trimmed to fit inside the bread case. Sprinkle with paprika. Pour another 1/3 cup of the turkey mixture around the bread case. Makes 6 to 8 servings.

Deviled Turkey

This is made with cooked legs, thighs, wings, or thick slices of breast. The Gubbins Sauce is a sauce the British serve with grilled meats.

Melt 1/4 cup butter and mix in 1/2 teaspoon dry mustard, 1 tablespoon vinegar, 1 tablespoon Worcestershire, and a dash of cayenne. Rub this thoroughly into the meat (enough for 4 to 6 servings), and then dip the pieces in fine dry bread crumbs. Broil over charcoal or under the broiler until nicely brown, and serve with Gubbins Sauce.

Gubbins Sauce: Mix together 1/2 cup melted butter, 2 tablespoons prepared mustard, 2 tablespoons heavy cream, and salt and liquid hot-pepper seasoning to taste. Makes enough sauce for 4 to 6 servings.

Salads

"Sallets in general consist of certain esculent plants and herbs, improved by culture, industry, and the art of the gard'ner." Or so said John Evelyn in 1699. We protest his definition because we firmly believe that the art of the cook comes in there, too, even in the preparation of the omnipresent but nonetheless unsurpassed mixed green salad. For the greens not only have to be tender—the gardener's part—but they must be fresh, well washed and dried, and crisp, then dressed with the just-right amount of olive oil and fine vinegar, salt and pepper, and mixed so that there is just enough dressing to coat every leaf without even a drop extra. That is a culinary accomplishment, even if no cooking heat is involved.

But even the most perfect mixed green salad can become boring when it's served day in, day out. We can vary it, of course, by trying new olive oils, a different vinegar, a judicious use of herbs, or slivers of mysterious but savory things. But let's try other salads, some that can take the place of the green one, or compound ones of raw or cooked vegetables or meat, shellfish, or cheese, or even a combination of them all.

Salade Niçoise

A Salade Niçoise is served as a first course or main course luncheon salad in the south of France. It has many versions, the "Niçoise" in the title merely indicating that it originated in the Mediterranean city of Nice, but its usual ingredients are those given here.

1 head iceberg lettuce
4 small tomatoes, peeled and quartered
1 cup each cooked green beans and diced cooked potatoes
1 red onion, sliced thin and the slices halved
2 hard-cooked eggs, sliced
1 can (7 oz.) tuna
6 or 8 anchovy fillets
Italian-style black olives
French dressing

Slice lettuce and arrange it in a large shallow bowl. On it, in a symmetrical design, arrange tomatoes, beans, potatoes, onion slices, egg slices, and tuna. Garnish with anchovy fillets and a few olives. Just before serving, pour over French dressing. Makes 6 to 8 servings.

Canned mandarin oranges, drained and mixed with cole slaw, make a salad that is especially good with cold sliced turkey.

Duck and Orange Salad

This is a cold version of the famous *Caneton à l'Orange*. It is a good dish for a luncheon or buffet.

Roast a 6-pound duck in the oven or over charcoal. Oven roasting will take about 2½ hours at 325°; charcoal roasting will take less time—1½ to 2 hours if the fire is hot. Remove skin. (You can use the skin to make a delicious appetizer; simply cut it in pieces, crisp in the oven, and serve sprinkled with salt.)

Cool the duck and cut meat in fairly large pieces. Pour on ¼ cup French dressing and chill. Peel and slice 3 oranges, and thinly slice 1 sweet onion. Marinate together in ¼ cup French dressing. Arrange duck on a bed of shredded lettuce and watercress. Surround with the oranges. Cover the duck with ½ cup of mayonnaise to which 1 teaspoon grated orange peel has been added. Sprinkle with ¼ cup slivered toasted almonds. Makes about 6 servings.

Rice and Chicken Salad

Rice salads make a good extra dish for a buffet supper, and a hearty rice salad such as this one can serve as a main dish for a luncheon.

Cook 1 pound rice and combine with 3 cups diced cooked chicken or turkey, 1 cup slivered toasted almonds, and ½ cup finely minced onion. Dress with 1½ cups mayonnaise mixed with 3 tablespoons curry powder, ¼ cup soy, and 2 tablespoons vinegar. Chill. Makes 18 to 20 buffet servings.

Okra Salad

Try this unusual and delicious salad when fresh okra is in season.

Select small pods of okra and cook until tender. Drain and cool. Make a dressing with ⅓ cup olive oil, ⅓ cup bland salad oil, 3 tablespoons wine vinegar, ½ teaspoon salt, 2 teaspoons each minced fresh tarragon, chives, and parsley, and a good dash of cayenne or liquid hot-pepper seasoning. This makes enough dressing for about 1½ to 2 pounds of okra, which will make 6 to 8 servings.

Potato Salad with Sour Cream

A well-chilled, robust potato salad is doubtless among the most popular summertime dishes. Here is an especially good version.

2 pounds new potatoes
1 teaspoon each sugar and salt
½ teaspoon dry mustard
Freshly ground pepper
¼ cup vinegar
2 teaspoons caraway or dill seed (optional)
1 cucumber, sliced
2 cups (1 pint) sour cream
Lettuce
Paprika or finely minced sweet, red pepper

Boil potatoes; peel and slice thin. Mix together sugar, salt, mustard, a few grindings of pepper, vinegar, caraway or dill seed (if used), cucumber, and sour cream. Combine with potatoes, chill, put in a lettuce-lined bowl, and sprinkle with paprika or sweet red pepper. Makes about 6 servings.

Apple and Potato Salad

When cold roast pork is on the menu, try this apple and potato salad. Begin with a cup of hot soup, and you'll have a quick and nutritious meal for a busy day. This salad is good with other cold meats, too.

Combine 2 cups diced cooked potatoes, 2 cups diced unpeeled red apples, ¼ cup minced onion, enough mayonnaise to blend (about ½ cup), and salt and pepper to taste; arrange on lettuce. Accompany with hot toasted shredded wheat crackers and Roquefort cheese. Makes 4 to 6 servings.

Insalata di Patate e Fagiolini

Potato and bean salad, a great favorite in Italy, can be varied in as many ways as a cook has imagination. This salad is an especially good accompaniment to meats cooked on the barbecue.

1 pound potatoes
¼ cup olive oil
1 tablespoon vinegar
Salt and pepper
½ pound green beans, cut in 1-inch pieces
2 tablespoons minced onion
Fillets of anchovies (optional)
Capers (optional)
Additional olive oil and vinegar

Cook potatoes until just tender; peel, and dice. Cover with the ¼ cup olive oil, the 1 tablespoon vinegar, ½ teaspoon salt, and some pepper. Cool. Cook beans until just tender. Add onion and, if you wish, a few fillets of anchovies and some capers. Combine with the potatoes, add enough more olive oil and vinegar to moisten well, add salt and pepper to taste, and mix carefully. Serve chilled. Makes about 6 servings.

Orange Salad

Tarragon adds unusual and refreshing flavor to orange salad.

Arrange peeled slices of navel oranges on lettuce leaves, sprinkle with minced fresh tarragon, and dress with plain French dressing. Serve well chilled.

Italian Green Bean and Tuna Salad

A salad that comes from Italy uses tuna in combination with herbs and tender green beans. Leave the beans whole if they are small ones; otherwise, slice them diagonally. This is particularly good with roast lamb or veal.

Cook 1 ½ pounds beans until tender-crisp. While they are still hot, dress with the following dressing: Mix together ¼ cup wine vinegar; 1 teaspoon each marjoram, sweet basil, tarragon, and chopped parsley; 2 green onions, chopped; ½ can tuna (7 oz. size); ¼ cup olive oil; 1 clove garlic, pressed; and 4 chopped anchovies. Let stand for 5 or 6 hours before serving. Makes 6 servings.

Tomatoes with Whipped Cream

This may strike you as a strange combination. It's nevertheless delicious—and a fine accompaniment to charcoal-grilled liver, beef, or fish.

Peel medium-sized tomatoes, remove cores, and place upside down on salad plates lined with lettuce. Over them pour a sauce made by combining 1 cup cream, whipped, 1 tablespoon prepared horseradish, and ¼ teaspoon salt. Serve at once. This is enough sauce for 6 to 8 servings.

Rice and Shrimp Salad

Here's a salad that would be an attractive addition to the buffet table, or it's filling enough to make a summer meal.

Combine 2 cups cooked rice with 2 cups cut-up cooked shrimp, 1 ½ cups cooked peas, 1 ½ cups sliced celery, ½ cup French dressing, 1 teaspoon salt, and either 1 teaspoon curry powder or ½ teaspoon dried dill weed. Mix well, put in lettuce cups, and sprinkle with ½ cup chopped salted peanuts or almonds. Makes 8 to 10 servings.

Jajek

Cucumber salad is popular in Middle East countries. This version is from Turkey.

Peel 5 slender cucumbers, cut in quarters lengthwise, discard seeds, and slice very thin. Sprinkle with 1 teaspoon salt. Mix together until smooth 1 cup yogurt, 1½ teaspoons vinegar in which 1 crushed clove of garlic has stood for about 1 hour (discard garlic), and ½ teaspoon dill weed (or 1 teaspoon minced fresh dill). Combine yogurt mixture with cucumbers, and put in a glass bowl to serve. Sprinkle with 1 tablespoon minced fresh mint and serve cold. Makes 6 servings.

Raw artichoke hearts, sliced very thin and marinated in a lemony French dressing, are a delicious addition to a salad. Dip the knife in lemon juice as you peel and slice, and drop slices into the dressing at once.

Salade Aixoise

As the name implies, this salad comes from the French town of Aix, where it is served as a first course or luncheon dish. It can be varied to suit your taste.

First line a large round plate or tray with lettuce, then arrange the following in concentric circles: quartered canned or cooked artichoke bottoms, cubed boiled and peeled potatoes, cooked or canned green beans, sliced fresh green and/or red peppers, peeled and quartered fresh tomatoes. Garnish with ripe olives and anchovy fillets and sprinkle with minced parsley. Dress with a mixture of 4 parts olive oil, 1 part tarragon vinegar, with salt and pepper to taste.

Turkey Salad

Leftover turkey stars in this salad.

For each quart of cut-up turkey meat, make the following dressing: Heat ⅓ cup olive oil with 12 finely-chopped anchovies, 1 tablespoon each capers, chopped parsley, and green onion, ½ cup lemon juice, and ¼ cup red wine vinegar. While hot, pour over cut-up turkey; chill overnight, and serve in lettuce cups, garnished with olives.

Bean Sprout Salad

Although the Chinese don't serve salads as such, they do have some interesting vegetables and fruits that can be used to make delicious and unusual salads. Fresh bean sprouts form the foundation of this salad. It is especially good with roast pork or broiled chicken.

Make a dressing of ½ teaspoon grated fresh ginger, 2 tablespoons soy sauce, 4 tablespoons salad oil, 1 tablespoon vinegar, and a little fresh puréed garlic (optional). Mix with this 1 pound fresh bean sprouts and arrange in a mound on a round dish. Sprinkle the top with ¼ cup slivered almonds, and surround the sprouts with drained, canned litchi nuts and melon balls. Serve very cold. This will be enough for 6 servings if it is a separate course, for 8 or 10 if it is a buffet dish.

Bohemian Cole Slaw

Here is a new version of this popular any-season salad.

Finely shred 1 pound cabbage (about ½ small head), sprinkle with about 1 tablespoon salt and put under a weighted plate for 3 hours; drain thoroughly. Mix together ¼ cup mild cider vinegar, ¼ cup heavy cream, 2 tablespoons salad oil or mayonnaise, 1½ to 2 teaspoons crushed caraway seed (do them in a mortar), a few grindings of pepper, and 1 cup sour cream. Combine this with 2 unpeeled red apples, shredded, and the cabbage. Add salt to taste if necessary, and serve. Makes 6 servings.

Litchi and Avocado Salad

Here's a good way to dress up avocado halves for a delicious first-course salad or buffet dish.

Chill 1 can (1 lb., 4 oz.) litchi nuts; drain, saving liquid, and dice the litchi nuts. Cut 6 ripe avocados in halves; remove pits. Mix litchi nuts with a dressing made by combining ¼ cup lemon juice, ¼ cup liquid drained from the litchi nuts, ¼ cup salad oil, 2 tablespoons soy sauce, and 2 teaspoons grated fresh ginger (optional). Fill avocado halves with the mixture and serve at once. Makes 12 servings.

Antipasto Salad

This combination of salad and antipasto course is just right to serve before pasta.

Chop 1 large, seeded green pepper, 8 radishes, 1 peeled and seeded cucumber, 3 peeled and seeded tomatoes, 1 heart of celery, 4 green onions, and 10 pitted ripe olives. Mix with ½ cup olive oil, 2 or 3 tablespoons red wine vinegar, 1 teaspoon salt, and some freshly ground pepper. Arrange in a lettuce-lined bowl or on individual plates, and garnish with chopped hard-cooked eggs and rolled anchovies. Makes 6 servings.

Insalata di Cipolle

This is an Italian onion salad that goes very well with any simple roast.

Peel and slice 6 large mild onions and cover with water. Add ½ teaspoon salt and simmer until tender yet still crisp; drain and cool. Dress with ½ cup olive oil, 3 to 5 tablespoons of red wine vinegar (according to your taste), ¾ teaspoon salt, ¼ teaspoon oregano, and a little fresh ground pepper. Chill, sprinkle with ¼ cup minced parsley, and serve without lettuce. Makes 6 to 8 servings.

Syrian Salad

A Syrian salad called *tabbouleh* or *tabbuli* would be an interesting addition to any buffet. Its base is *bulghour*, an Armenian cracked wheat cereal, but it can be made with the quick-cooking cracked wheat found in most American markets. In Middle East countries, this is finger food; the tabbouleh is placed in the center of the table and everyone helps himself, scooping up the mixture with the crisp leaves.

- 1 cup bulghour or quick-cooking cracked wheat
- 1 bunch each fresh mint and parsley, chopped fine (about 1 cup each chopped mint and parsley)
- ½ cup chopped green onions
- 1 pound tomatoes, peeled, seeded, and chopped
- ⅓ cup each lemon juice and olive oil
- Salt and pepper to taste
- Romaine or tender cabbage leaves

Soak wheat in warm (not hot) water for 1 hour. Drain well, pressing out water. Add chopped mint and parsley, green onions, tomatoes, lemon juice, and olive oil. Add salt and pepper to taste. Heap in center of a large round plate, and surround with young leaves of romaine or tender cabbage leaves. Makes 6 to 8 servings.

Artichoke-stuffed Tomatoes

Ripe red tomatoes make a fine first course for a party dinner. Select tomatoes of uniform size, and allow one for each person.

Peel tomatoes or not, as you please, cut a slice from the top, and scoop out the pulp. Sprinkle with salt, and drain upside down. Stuff each tomato with an artichoke heart that has been marinated in French dressing. Arrange them on lettuce leaves, and pour over a dressing made by combining 1 cup mayonnaise with 1 teaspoon anchovy paste and 1 teaspoon garlic vinegar. Garnish with crossed anchovy fillets.

Cold Beef Salad

In France this is called *boeuf vinaigrette*, in Mexico, *carne a la vinagreta*, and in Italy a similar dish is called *manzo lesso, salsa verde*. Any of these versions is a fine way to use up leftover beef, whether boiled or roasted. The Mexican way is perhaps the simplest.

Cut the cooked meat in slices or strips and put in a deep platter. For each pound of meat, slice 1 large onion thin; cover meat with onion slices, then sprinkle with 2 tablespoons each of capers and minced parsley, and 1 teaspoon minced oregano. Mix together ½ cup olive oil, ¼ cup wine vinegar, 1 teaspoon prepared mustard, and ½ teaspoon salt. Pour over the meat and let stand for 3 hours before chilling. Makes 6 servings.

Cucumber and Spinach Salad

This interesting salad has an Armenian ancestry. It's especially good with lamb or mutton.

Combine 2 peeled and diced cucumbers (discard seeds, if large); 1 cup sliced celery; ½ cup each minced parsley, quartered green olives, quartered ripe olives, and pine nuts. Tear 2 bunches raw spinach into pieces, discarding stems; combine with other ingredients. Make dressing of ½ cup olive oil, ¼ cup red wine vinegar, 1 teaspoon salt, some freshly ground black pepper, and a pinch of oregano. Makes 6 to 8 servings.

Lobster or chicken salad, served in tender pastry shells instead of nested in lettuce, is very nice for buffet service. Sprinkle the tops with toasted slivered almonds.

Hearts of Palm Salad

If you want a light salad that is a little different, try this one: Slice hearts of palm, arrange on a bed of lettuce, and dress with a classic French dressing of oil and vinegar, salt and pepper. One can of hearts of palm will serve 8 to 10 persons.

Salade de Fromage

There are no greens in this salad, made famous at Androuillet, the noted Paris cheese house. Any firm cheese or combination of cheeses can be substituted for the Swiss cheese. The sprinkling of minced parsley is not authentic, but we like the added color and flavor. And there's no reason why the salad shouldn't be served in nests of lettuce, if you wish.

Dice ½ pound of Swiss cheese in ¼-inch cubes. Combine them with 1 cup mayonnaise, 1 chopped hard-cooked egg, and 1 teaspoon (or more) prepared mustard. Sprinkle with minced parsley. Makes 4 to 6 servings.

Onion and Cheese Salad

Cheese, ham, green pepper, and onion slices give this salad attractive color as well as refreshing flavor and texture contrasts.

Slice a large sweet onion very thin, cut slices in half, separate rings, and cover with ice water. Chill for about 2 hours. Cut into matchlike pieces ¼ pound Swiss cheese, ¼ pound cooked ham, and 1 large green pepper; combine with drained onion. Stir in 3 tablespoons wine vinegar, ⅓ cup salad oil (part olive oil for flavor), salt, and freshly ground pepper to taste. Chill. Serve on lettuce. Makes 6 servings.

Homemade Mayonnaise

It's almost impossible to buy mayonnaise that is not sweetened, or mayonnaise made with olive oil. But you can make your own in a matter of minutes if you use an electric blender.

Put into the blender 2 tablespoons lemon juice, ½ teaspoon salt, 1 teaspoon prepared mustard, 1 whole egg, and ¼ cup oil—olive oil or part olive oil, or all salad oil, as you prefer. Cover and flip switch to high. While blender is going, remove cover or center disk and slowly add ¾ cup more of the oil. It will immediately thicken into a smooth, creamy mayonnaise. Makes 1¼ cups.

Sauces Relishes & Seasonings

Although sauces are an important part of *haute cuisine*, they are not necessarily rich, elaborate, or French. Melted butter and lemon juice is a sauce; so is the gravy for a pot roast. The lore of sauces, the basic ones and the many variations, is a fascinating one, and we hope the recipes here will arouse so much interest that beginning cooks will pursue the subject further. But even if such is not the case, those recipes included in this chapter should add interest to any cook's meals.

The subject of seasonings, too, is a complex one, including as it does herbs, spices, and mixtures made from one or both of them. Some are subtle, some assertive, but all should be added with finesse and discretion. We merely touch upon their uses, but we believe that the recipe for *quatre épices* alone will be a joy to any cook who takes the little time required to make a batch.

As for relishes, the recipes for them are limited to a few unusual ones for chutneys and the like.

Sauce à l'Ambassadrice

This may seem like a fancy name for raisin sauce, but it's a very special raisin sauce, good with ham, tongue, or pork of any kind.

Combine 1 cup Sauce Espagnole (page 155) or brown beef gravy, 1 tablespoon each currant jelly and lemon juice, a dash of cayenne, and salt, if needed. Put over low heat to simmer for 5 minutes. Meanwhile put ½ cup seeded raisins in a strainer, pour 1 quart boiling water over them, and add raisins to sauce. Bring to a boil and serve.

Khyaar bi Laban

The Arabs use *laban* (Lebanese for yogurt) any number of ways. Here it is combined with cucumbers and mint in a sauce that is delicious with grilled meats or fish.

Combine 2 cups yogurt with 1 cup peeled, seeded, and finely diced cucumber; set aside. Put 2 cloves garlic through a press or mash in a mortar with ½ teaspoon salt. Thoroughly mix with 1 tablespoon yogurt and add 1 tablespoon finely minced mint. Combine the two mixtures; garnish with sprigs of mint.

Soubise Sauce

This is a French classic, good with lamb or mutton chops or with boiled beef.

Chop 2 medium-sized onions and cook them in a little water until very tender. Drain and press them through a sieve. Mix with ¼ cup heavy cream, 2 tablespoons butter or margarine, salt and pepper to taste, and a grating of fresh nutmeg. Serve hot.

Sauce Piquante

Try this with fresh boiled tongue.

Chop 1 small onion and cook it in 2 tablespoons butter until wilted. To this add 3 tablespoons vinegar (preferably tarragon vinegar), 1 cup beef gravy (the canned kind will do nicely), 1 tablespoon minced parsley, and a dash of liquid hot-pepper seasoning. Heat, and just before serving, add 4 small pickled gherkins, sliced paper-thin.

Mustard Sauce

A robust mustard sauce made with sour cream is especially good with boiled potatoes and boiled beef tongue or corned beef.

Combine 1 cup sour cream with ¼ cup mayonnaise, 2 tablespoons prepared mustard, a few drops of garlic juice (use a press, or grate the garlic), and 1 tablespoon prepared horseradish.

It is no wonder that powdered Spanish saffron is one of the world's most expensive spices when you consider that it takes over 75,000 blossoms to make one pound of powdered saffron. Fortunately, though, a little goes a long way, as it has both intense color and intense flavor.

Tarragon Sauce

Here's a different sauce to try with asparagus.

Mash 2 tablespoons each of minced fresh parsley, chives, and tarragon in a mortar. (Or use 1½ teaspoons dried tarragon.) Add 1 cup melted butter, 2 teaspoons lemon juice, and 2 slices crisp toast, crushed into crumbs. This makes enough for 3 pounds of asparagus.

Aioli

Garlic lovers will love this sauce of Provence. Serve it with steamed fish—any firm-fleshed white variety.

Put 4 large garlic cloves through a garlic press, and mix well with the raw yolks of 2 eggs. Add ½ teaspoon salt, and drip in ½ cup olive oil, a little at a time, stirring until it becomes thick like mayonnaise.

Marinara Sauce

Here's a sauce that's good with spaghetti, polenta, gnocchi, or any pasta. You'll probably have to visit an Italian market for the special pack of Italian tomatoes called for in the recipe, but it's worth this extra effort. The recipe may be varied with the addition of minced clams, broiled slices of Italian sausage, cooked shrimp, or mushrooms. It makes about 3 pints, but it freezes nicely and is handy to have on hand.

¼ pound bacon
½ cup olive oil
4 large onions, chopped
3 large cloves garlic, puréed or very finely minced
2 large cans (about 2 lb., 3 oz. each) Italian peeled plum tomatoes with basil
¼ cup minced parsley
6 chopped anchovies
An herb bouquet (1 bay leaf, 3 whole cloves, a pinch of thyme, and 1 teaspoon basil, tied together in cheesecloth)
Salt and freshly ground pepper to taste

Chop bacon and cook until it begins to crisp. Add olive oil, onions, and garlic. Cook until the onions are soft, then add tomatoes, parsley, anchovies, and the herb bouquet. Simmer very slowly for an hour. Discard herbs. Force sauce through a strainer or whirl smooth in a blender (a little at a time). Season to taste with salt and pepper. Before using, simmer again for 20 minutes or so.

Sauce Gribiche

This sauce can be served with any cold fish or shellfish, or with brains, tongue, and many cold vegetables. It can also be used as a salad dressing.

3 hard-cooked eggs
½ teaspoon salt
1 teaspoon dry mustard
¼ teaspoon black pepper
½ cup wine vinegar
¾ cup each olive oil and salad oil
½ cup chopped sour pickles
2 teaspoons each minced parsley, tarragon, and chives

Remove yolks from eggs and press them through a sieve. Mix with the salt, mustard, pepper, vinegar, olive oil and salad oil, pickles, parsley, tarragon, and chives. Finely chop the egg whites and mix in.

Ten-second Hollandaise Sauce

Ten seconds after you flick the blender switch, you have this smooth, creamy Hollandaise. Since it isn't cooked, but is only heated by the warmth of the butter and the blender container, it will not curdle.

3 egg yolks
1½ tablespoons lemon juice
¾ cup melted butter
1 tablespoon hot water
½ teaspoon salt
Dash of cayenne
1 teaspoon prepared mustard

Let egg yolks and lemon juice stand (separately) at room temperature for at least 2 hours before using. Heat blender container with hot running water. Leave 1 tablespoon hot water in the bottom. Add egg yolks and turn on blender. Pour in warm melted butter in a steady stream. Toss in salt, cayenne, mustard, and the lemon juice. Stop the blender, and serve at once. Makes 2 cups sauce. (You can reheat leftover sauce in the top of a double boiler over hot but not boiling water; stir until smooth.)

Anchovy Sauce

A simple anchovy sauce, particularly good on charcoal-broiled salmon or other fish, is made by adding 1 tablespoon anchovy paste, 1 tablespoon lemon juice, and a dash of liquid hot-pepper seasoning to ¼ pound melted butter.

Béchamel Sauce

Béchamel Sauce, or Cream Sauce, is used regularly in creamed dishes and casseroles. Seasonings may be added as desired to bring out the flavor of a particular food.

4 tablespoons butter or margarine
4 tablespoons flour
1 cup rich chicken stock
1 cup light cream
Salt and grated nutmeg to taste

Cook butter and flour together for 2 to 3 minutes to remove the flour's raw taste. Stir in chicken stock and cream; stirring constantly, cook until smooth and thick. Season with salt and nutmeg. When serving with fish, substitute fish stock for chicken stock.

Mornay Sauce

Combine 1 cup Béchamel Sauce with 2 tablespoons each grated Parmesan cheese and grated Swiss cheese, and a dash of cayenne. Heat just until the cheese is melted.

Rémoulade Sauce

This sauce has many variations and many uses. Originally, it was plain mayonnaise made with cooked egg yolks instead of raw ones. The word comes from the French *rémoudre* (to grind) because the eggs were ground in a mortar. Today some rémoulades, such as the New Orleans version, are hot with mustard and even horseradish, others are seasoned with anchovies or anchovy paste, and still others have mixed vegetables added. Here is one version that is good with shrimp or lobster as an appetizer, or as a dunk for raw vegetables.

Combine 1 cup mayonnaise, 2 or 3 chopped shallots or green onions, 2 minced anchovy fillets, 1 teaspoon chopped capers, 1 chopped gherkin (not a sweet one), and 1 tablespoon minced parsley.

Quick Béarnaise Sauce

You can make a quick Sauce Béarnaise by whirling ingredients in a blender.

Soak 1 teaspoon dry tarragon in 1 tablespoon tarragon vinegar. Add 1 cup mayonnaise, ⅛ teaspoon dry mustard, and 3 peeled shallots or green onions; whirl in blender.

Mirepoix

This is widely used in French *haute cuisine* as a base for some sauces and for braising. It's easy to make and freezes nicely.

Melt 6 tablespoons butter in a heavy saucepan. Add ½ pound finely diced raw ham, 2 minced carrots, 2 chopped onions, 2 minced shallots (optional), 6 sprigs parsley and 1 rib celery (minced), ½ teaspoon thyme, and 1 bay leaf. Brown lightly; add 1 cup white wine and 6 crushed peppercorns. Simmer for 30 minutes; remove bay leaf. Put into a covered jar and freeze or store in refrigerator. Use for adding flavor to soups, sauces, and stews, and to the liquid used in braising. Salt when used, and add in amounts to achieve desired flavor.

Pesto

In Genoa they use pesto on pastas and on gnocchi. It may also be used as a flavoring for soup, and it's delicious spread on toasted French bread and served with charcoal-broiled meats. Covered and refrigerated, it will last for many weeks.

Wash fresh basil and shake dry. Pick leaves from stems; measure 1 cup of leaves, firmly packed. Put in a mortar or an electric blender along with 6 large cloves of garlic (peeled), ½ pound of freshly grated Parmesan cheese, and ¼ cup pine nuts. Pound or whirl, adding olive oil drop by drop (you'll need about ½ cup of olive oil, perhaps a little more). The pesto should be the consistency of mayonnaise.

Fresh Herb Bouquet

Many recipes use an herb bouquet, often called *bouquet garni.* For a simple fresh herb bouquet, use 3 or 4 sprigs of parsley, 1 bay leaf (if large, use half a leaf), and 2 sprigs of thyme. Bind the herbs together with a coarse white cotton thread or fine cotton twine.

You can vary herb bouquets by adding 4 or 5 chives (for fish), a sprig of marjoram (for chicken), a sprig of basil (for tomato dishes), or a small sprig of rosemary (for beef or lamb).

Dried Herb Bouquet

You can make an herb bouquet with dried herbs if you don't have fresh ones. Tie the herbs in a little cheesecloth bag, with a string long enough to make removal from the pan easy. They'll keep on the pantry shelf.

Mix together ½ cup dried parsley and ¼ cup dried thyme as the basic mixture for the dried herb bouquets. For each bouquet, place 1 teaspoon of this mixture on a 3-inch square of cheesecloth (double thickness) along with ¼ of a bay leaf. Gather up the sides of the cheesecloth and tie, leaving a 6-inch length of thread for easy handling.

Here are some suggestions for varying dried herb bouquets: For seafood, add 2 tablespoons dried lemon peel to the basic mixture and put 2 peppercorns in each bouquet. For brown stock, add 1 whole clove, 2 peppercorns, and a small piece of dried mace to each bouquet. For tomato soups and sauces, add 1 tablespoon oregano and 2 tablespoons dried basil to the basic mixture, as well as adding 1 clove and 2 peppercorns to each bouquet.

Glacé de Viande

Meat glaze, or *glacé de viande*, is often called for in very elegant recipes. It is excellent, too, for adding strength to soups, sauces, and ragouts.

Put a pint or more of greaseless cleared stock or canned beef bouillon in a heavy saucepan and simmer until it becomes so thick it coats a spoon. Pour into a sterilized jar and keep in the refrigerator or freezer until needed.

Quatre Épices

The French keep this mixture of four spices on hand to add zest to soups, salads, sauces, or anything else that needs it.

Combine ¼ cup freshly ground white pepper, 1 tablespoon freshly ground ginger, 1 tablespoon grated nutmeg (grate it yourself), and 1 ¼ teaspoons freshly ground cloves. (To assure freshness, purchase a new jar of the ginger and of the cloves.) Mix well, sift, and put in a jar. Keep in a cool, dark place—the refrigerator is ideal.

Quick Espagnole Sauce

This classic brown sauce may be quickly made with canned bouillon or bouillon cubes.

- 1 cup each diced, lean, cooked ham and chopped onions
- ½ cup each sliced celery and sliced carrots
- 2 large tomatoes, peeled and chopped
- ¼ cup butter
- ¼ cup flour
- 1 quart beef stock
- 1 herb bouquet (parsley, bay, thyme)
- ½ cup sherry

Cook ham, onions, celery, carrots, and tomatoes in butter until vegetables are soft. Stir in flour and cook for 2 minutes. Pour in stock (1 quart water and 6 bouillon cubes, or equivalent in canned bouillon, may be used). Add herb bouquet. Simmer gently for 1 hour. Remove herb bouquet and add sherry. Cool. Skim off fat and refrigerate or freeze. Makes 5 cups.

Sauce Diable

Use this for turkey, beef ribs, chicken, or other meats, which have been cooked, dipped in a mixture of melted butter and vinegar, rolled in fine crumbs, and grilled.

Cook together 1 cup dry white wine, 2 tablespoons chopped onion, a small piece of bay leaf, and a pinch of thyme until liquid is reduced one-half. Combine with 1 cup Espagnole Sauce, 1 tablespoon prepared mustard, 2 tablespoons wine vinegar, and a little cayenne. Serve hot.

Duxelles

This is a basic ingredient used by the French in many ways, but especially for stuffing vegetables, or as a basis for Sauce Duxelles. Because it can be made with mushroom stems, and keeps a long time, it is a good addition to any adventurous cook's repertoire.

Cook 2 tablespoons minced shallots or green onions in 2 tablespoons each butter and bland oil. Add ½ pound finely minced mushrooms or mushroom stems, and cook slowly until moisture has evaporated. Add 1 teaspoon minced parsley, and salt and pepper to taste. Makes 1 ¼ cups. This is called dry Duxelles, or *Duxelles Sèche*.

To use for stuffing vegetables, put ¼ cup of Duxelles Sèche in a saucepan with 3 tablespoons white wine, and simmer until the wine has evaporated. Add 1 tablespoon tomato purée or sauce, 1 tablespoon beef extract, half a small clove garlic, pressed, and 3 tablespoons bread crumbs. Correct seasoning, and if too soupy, simmer until the right consistency. Use for stuffing small tomatoes, mushrooms, or tiny patty pan squash.

To make Sauce Duxelles, cook ¾ cup white wine until reduced one-half; add ¼ cup tomato purée, ¼ cup Duxelles Sèche, and 2 cups of bouillon which has been reduced from 4 cups. Simmer for 6 minutes, then add 2 teaspoons minced parsley, and serve with croquettes or any breaded, fried meat.

Salsa Picante

If you like a hot sauce for shrimp or other seafood cocktails, you'll like this South American version of rémoulade.

To 1 cup mayonnaise, add 2 teaspoons grated fresh horseradish or prepared horseradish, 2 teaspoons prepared mustard, 1 tablespoon chopped capers, 1 teaspoon each minced chives and parsley, and ½ teaspoon anchovy paste. Mix well, and if it's still not hot enough, add liquid hot-pepper seasoning to taste.

Papaya Chutney

This is a quick and easy uncooked chutney that is delicious with curry. Add more ginger or chili, if you wish.

Select a large, not too ripe papaya; peel, seed, and grate it coarsely. Mix with 1 tablespoon finely grated ginger, 1 small clove garlic crushed to a paste with 1 teaspoon salt, 1 tablespoon lemon juice, 1 chopped canned green chili, and ½ cup grated coconut (preferably fresh). Makes 2 cups.

Quick Chutney

Here's a chutney, with an intriguing flavor, that can be made in a matter of minutes.

Heat 2 tablespoons butter in a small pan, then add 1 teaspoon whole mustard seed. Shake over the fire until the seeds start to pop. Add 1 cup grated coconut (fresh or dried), and 1 can (4 oz.) peeled green chilies, rinsed of their seeds and chopped. Cook over low heat for 3 minutes, stirring. Mash mixture in a mortar; add 1 cup yogurt. Season with salt to taste and ½ teaspoon curry powder. Serve cold.

Date Chutney

This is easy to make and delicious. It keeps for two or three weeks in the refrigerator, or it can be frozen.

- 1 cup each sugar and vinegar
- 1½ pounds dates, pitted
- 2 to 4 cloves garlic, peeled
- 1 large piece (about ½ oz.) fresh ginger
- 6 to 10 small dried hot red chili peppers, seeded
- 1 teaspoon salt
- ½ cup slivered blanched almonds

Combine sugar and vinegar and simmer for 5 minutes. Grind dates along with garlic, ginger, and chili peppers. Combine date mixture with syrup; add salt and almonds. Mix well and put in a jar. Makes about 2½ cups.

Shrimp Sambal

This is a good condiment to serve with curry.

Chop 1 cup cooked or canned shrimp and cook it in 2 tablespoons butter for a few minutes. Add 2 tablespoons grated fresh coconut or chopped flaked coconut, 2 finely minced or pressed cloves of garlic, 1 chopped peeled green chili, and 1 tablespoon lime juice. Mix well, season with salt, and serve.

Asiers

These Danish pickles are almost a must with a Danish meal.

For 8 pints of asiers, select 16 long thin cucumbers with few small seeds. Peel them, cut in quarters lengthwise, then cut each piece in half crosswise. Remove seeds and discard. Sprinkle with ¼ cup salt and let stand overnight. Boil together 1 quart white vinegar, 2 tablespoons salt, 2 teaspoons mustard seed, ½ teaspoon black peppercorns, and 1 cup sugar for 5 minutes. Drain cucumbers and dry. Pack in hot sterilized pint jars; in each jar, put 1 chili pequin and 1 sprig of dill (if unavailable, add 1 tablespoon dill weed to the brine while cooking it). Pour in brine, filling the jars, and seal while hot.

Curried Peaches

Serve these with ham, chicken, turkey, or spareribs.

Drain 1 large can (1 lb., 13 oz.) cling peaches and arrange cut side up in a baking dish. Combine ¼ cup each butter and brown sugar, 1 tablespoon curry powder, and a few grains of salt. Divide among the cavities of the peaches, pour ½ cup of the peach syrup in the pan, and bake in a moderate oven (350°) for 15 minutes. Serve hot or warm.

Tarragon Pickled Beets

These add piquancy to meat and fish dishes.

Drain 1 can (1 lb., 4 oz.) whole baby beets, saving half the liquid. To the beet liquid, add ¼ cup tarragon vinegar, 1 teaspoon sugar, and 1 small clove garlic, cut in half; bring to a boil. Pour over the beets and chill for 12 hours. Remove garlic before serving.

Breads & Sandwiches

This chapter is a bit of a hodgepodge, but, we hope, a hodgepodge of recipes you will treasure. It is a potpourri of unusual breads and breadstuffs, and sandwiches that are not run-of-the-mill. There are yeast breads, toasts, crumpets, bagels, and foreign breads.

Here are recipes to fit many occasions. Some are good as appetizers or to serve with soups or salads, others as breakfast or brunch dishes; there are robust breads that make wonderful barbecue accompaniments, breads that can star on a luncheon menu, sandwiches hearty enough to be supper dishes.

The recipes come from a variety of sources. Some are from far away places, some are adaptations of home favorites, and some are our own concoctions. These are breads that are fun to make and that will delight your family or guests. Of them all, there is no one that can't be varied or changed or transformed into something completely different. It is, in fact, our hope that you'll experiment, for only in that way can new recipes be added to our great American cuisine.

Sesame French Toast

This variation of French toast, served with chicken livers in cream, makes a festive brunch dish.

For each 2 pieces of bread allow 1 slightly beaten egg, a pinch of salt, and ¼ cup milk. Dip bread slices in a mixture of the egg, salt, and milk, then sprinkle one side thickly with sesame seed. Melt butter in frying pan; using a wide spatula, place bread in pan with sesame seed side down. Sprinkle top with sesame seed before turning. When brown on both sides, transfer to a hot platter, top each slice with a curl of crisp bacon, and surround with chicken livers in cream (page 129).

Baking powder biscuits, to which curry has been added, are particularly good with lamb stew or with creamed tuna or other creamed dishes. Simply add 1 teaspoon curry powder to each cup of flour or mix used, and bake as usual.

Thousand Layer Buns

Whoever named these was an expert in hyperbole, but these Chinese buns are nonetheless delicious and great fun to make.

Dissolve 1 package yeast (active dry or compressed) in 2 cups warm water (lukewarm for compressed yeast). Add 1 tablespoon each of sugar, salt, and bland oil (such as peanut or corn oil). Stir in 3 cups sifted flour, turn out on a floured board, and knead in another 3 cups sifted flour. Put in an oiled bowl, turn dough over so that the top will also be oiled, and cover. Let rise in a warm spot until nearly double in bulk. Punch down. Pinch off 8 pieces of dough, and form into balls 2 inches in diameter (about 1¼ ounces each).

Divide remaining dough into ½-ounce pieces, and form into smaller balls, 1¼ inches in diameter. On a floured board roll the smaller balls into rounds about 2½ inches in diameter, and wrap each stack of 8 rounds in a large pancake, rolled from the 2-inch pieces of dough, completely enclosing the stack. Gather edges and pinch firmly together at the bottom. Put each bun on a square of oiled paper and allow to rise for 1 hour. Steam for 20 minutes. Serve hot.

Pecan Garlic Bread

Guests will be pleasantly surprised when you serve this unusual pecan garlic bread.

Cream together ¼ pound butter, ½ cup very finely minced parsley, ½ cup finely chopped pecans, 1 small clove garlic, purèed, and a pinch of salt. Slice 2 medium-sized loaves of French bread almost to the bottom crust, and spread with this mixture. This is delicious unheated, but warm it if you prefer.

Spiral Bread

Whether you begin with a hot roll mix or your own recipe for homemade bread, you'll find this spiral loaf easy to make. It's especially good served warm.

Prepare 1 package (14 oz.) hot roll mix or dough for 1 loaf (5 by 9 inches) of bread. Let rise as usual; punch down and roll out on a lightly floured board into a rectangle 8 inches wide and as long as it becomes when rolled ¼-inch thick. Brush with 1 slightly beaten egg (saving egg that remains), then spread evenly with any of the suggested fillings below or with your own concoction.

Roll like a jelly roll, starting at a narrow end and pulling and stretching the dough slightly as you roll. Seal edges by pinching; place seam side down in a buttered loaf pan. Brush top with melted butter and let rise in a warm place for 1 hour, or until almost double in bulk. Bake in a hot oven (400°) for 50 minutes, or until nicely browned.

Parsley and Onion Filling: Cook 1 cup minced parsley and 1 cup minced green onions in 2 tablespoons butter until soft, about 3 minutes. Season with about 1½ teaspoons salt, and a dash each of ground pepper and any favorite herb. Mix with beaten egg remaining from bread recipe.

Sesame Filling: Cook 1 cup sesame seed and 1 cup chopped onion in 2 tablespoons butter until the seeds are lightly browned. Season with ½ teaspoon salt and a dash of pepper, and add egg remaining from bread recipe.

Cheese and Poppy Seed Filling: Toast ½ cup poppy seed in a dry frying pan, shaking to keep seeds from burning. Combine with 1¼ cups shredded Cheddar cheese, 1 tablespoon soft butter, a dash of liquid hot-pepper seasoning, ½ teaspoon salt, and the egg remaining from the bread recipe. (About ¼ cup chopped green onion may be added to this mixture.)

Swedish Rye Bread

This recipe makes a wonderfully moist rye bread, good for sandwiches, for smörebrod, or toasted for breakfast.

- 1 package yeast (active dry or compressed)
- ½ cup warm water (lukewarm for compressed yeast)
- ½ cup each dark molasses and shortening
- 1 tablespoon salt
- 2 cups boiling water
- 4 cups each sifted rye flour and sifted all-purpose flour

Dissolve yeast in the warm water. Mix together molasses, shortening, salt, and boiling water. Stir until the shortening is melted, and cool to lukewarm. Add yeast mixture and the rye flour, and beat well. Add white flour, and knead until smooth. Put into a well-greased bowl, then turn dough over so the top will be greased. Cover and let rise until almost double in bulk. Punch down, let rise for 30 minutes, then turn out on a lightly floured board and divide into 3 parts. Form into loaves, put in greased bread pans (5 by 9 inches), and let rise in a warm place until nearly double in bulk. Bake in a moderate oven (350°) for 40 minutes, or until browned.

Corn Chili Bread

This is a wonderfully rich moist bread that goes beautifully with hamburgers, or broiled chicken or steak.

- 3 ears fresh corn
- 1 cup yellow corn meal
- 1½ teaspoons salt
- 3 teaspoons baking powder
- 1 cup sour cream
- ⅔ cup melted butter or margarine
- 2 eggs, well beaten
- ¼ pound jack cheese, finely diced
- 1 can (4 oz.) peeled green chilies, rinsed of their seeds and cut in small pieces

Scrape kernels from corn. Combine with corn meal, salt, baking powder, sour cream, melted butter or margarine, eggs, cheese, and chilies. Pour into a well-greased, 9-inch square baking dish, and bake in a moderate oven (350°) for 1 hour. Makes 6 generous servings.

Crumpets

With this new and very easy recipe, crumpets are almost as easy to make as pancakes.

Combine ½ cup milk and ½ cup boiling water. Crumble 1 package yeast (active dry or compressed) into the mixture, then beat in 1 teaspoon sugar, 1 teaspoon salt, and 1¾ cups sifted flour. Let rise in a warm place until almost double in bulk and very bubbly, about 1 hour. Mix ¾ teaspoon soda in 1 tablespoon hot water, and beat into mixture. Again allow to rise until double in bulk.

Place a dozen 3 or 3¼-inch muffin rings on a moderately hot griddle. (You can use cans, the size used for tuna, with tops and bottoms removed.) Divide mixture among rings and cook until very dry and bubbly on top. Remove rings, turn, and brown on other side. Split the crumpets, toast, butter before serving. Makes 12.

Hungarian Bacon Biscuits

The Hungarian name for these yeast-raised biscuits is *Tö portyús pogacasa.*

- 1 package yeast, active dry or compressed
- ¼ cup warm water (lukewarm for compressed yeast)
- 1 teaspoon each salt, sugar, and freshly ground black pepper
- 2 eggs, beaten
- ½ cup sour cream
- 2½ cups sifted flour
- 1 pound bacon
- 1 egg yolk
- 1 tablespoon milk

Dissolve yeast in warm water. Add salt, sugar, pepper, eggs, sour cream, and flour. Turn out on a floured board and knead until smooth and satiny. Let dough rise in a greased bowl until double in bulk. Meanwhile, cook bacon until crisp; drain and crumble into small bits.

When dough is double in bulk, punch down, and mix in the bacon. Knead again to mix thoroughly, roll out ½-inch thick, and cut into 2-inch rounds with a biscuit cutter. Arrange on a buttered baking sheet and allow to rise for 30 minutes.

Slash top of each biscuit with 3 shallow diagonal cuts. Brush biscuits with egg yolk beaten with the 1 tablespoon milk. Bake in a moderate oven (350°) for 15 to 20 minutes, or until nicely browned. Serve piping hot. Makes about 2 dozen.

Lahm Ajoun

The Armenians and Syrians make a bread that is akin to *pizza*—it is a yeast dough, rolled thin and round, and spread with a savory topping before it is baked. In its native land, it is eaten as a main dish, but it's also good as an appetizer or in place of a sandwich.

Use your favorite recipe to prepare enough yeast bread dough for 1 loaf, or use a package of hot roll mix. When the dough is ready to shape, break off pieces about 2 inches in diameter and form them into balls. Roll out the balls on a lightly floured board until you have thin pancake-like pieces about 6 inches in diameter. Arrange on cooky sheets and spread each piece with 3 tablespoons of lamb filling (see below), letting filling come to the edges. Bake in a hot oven (425°) for 20 minutes, or until the meat is cooked. Roll up before serving. Makes 24 to 30. (If you want to serve this as an appetizer, make pieces half this size.)

Filling: Grind together 1 pound lean lamb shoulder, 1 large onion, 2 cloves garlic, 1 large green pepper, and 1 cup chopped parsley (do not pack). Mix with 1 teaspoon salt, ½ teaspoon allspice, a little freshly ground pepper, and 2 cups chopped canned tomatoes.

Kluski

Kluski are Polish dumplings, and they are very good served with any ragout or pot roast, or with fricasseed chicken.

2 cups well-drained large curd cottage cheese
½ cup flour
2 teaspoons salt
2 eggs plus 1 egg yolk, beaten together
6 tablespoons melted butter
About 1 cup toasted bread crumbs
¼ cup butter

Combine cottage cheese, flour, salt, eggs, and the 6 tablespoons melted butter. Mix very well to make a soft smooth dough. Bring a pot of salted water to a boil and drop in batter by rounded teaspoonfuls, a few at a time. Skim off as they rise to the top. When all are made, roll them in toasted bread crumbs, and sauté in the ¼ cup butter in the same pan in which they are to be served.

Cheese Fingers

This is quick and easy. Serve the cheese fingers as an accompaniment for soups and salads.

Trim crusts from dry bread and cut each slice in thirds, making fingers. Add 1 puréed clove garlic and ½ teaspoon salt to 1 cup milk. Dip bread quickly in milk mixture, and roll thoroughly in grated Parmesan cheese. Arrange on baking sheet and bake in slow oven (300°) until crisp.

What we call French toast, the French call pain perdu, or "lost bread," and it's a dish that's at least five centuries old. Undoubtedly devised as a simple way to reclaim stale, or lost, bread, a recipe appears in the fifteenth century Harleian Manuscripts—"Payn per-dew," they call it. Interestingly, the Belgians call it pain trouvé, or "found bread."

Bagels

Bagels are fun to make and they are a good snack to serve with coffee, beer, or other drinks. They may be made regular size, using a standard doughnut cutter, or miniature size, using two smaller round cutters, one 1½ inches in diameter, one ½ inch for making the hole.

For about 18 large or 6 dozen small bagels, use a package of hot roll mix. Add 2 tablespoons of sugar to the mix, then follow directions on the package. After the first rising, turn out on a well-floured board and knead for 3 minutes. Cover and allow to rest for 15 minutes, then roll ⅜ to ½ inch thick for the large size, ¼ inch for the smaller one. Cut with doughnut cutter or smaller cutters, and let rise in a warm place until double in bulk. Drop, a few at a time, into a large pot of boiling water. When they rise to the surface, which will be almost at once, remove with a slotted spoon or spatula, and arrange on greased cooky sheets.

Bake in a hot oven (400°) until nicely browned. This will take up to 18 minutes for the large size, about 10 for the smaller ones. To serve, split, toast or not as you wish, spread with cream cheese, and then make a sandwich with smoked salmon (lox) as the filling.

Salt Sticks

Salt sticks seem to mean different things to different people, but to all they are noted not so much for their salt as for their caraway seeds. One way to make them is to use a recipe for a rich pie crust. Or they may be made from your favorite roll dough, or a package of roll mix.

To make salt sticks from a pie crust dough: Cut ⅓ cup each butter and shortening into 1 cup unsifted all-purpose flour; add 1 egg yolk and ½ teaspoon salt, then with a fork mix in about 1 tablespoon water. Chill dough, then roll balls of it under the fingers to make pencil-thick sticks. Cut into 2½-inch lengths, brush with 1 egg that has been lightly beaten with 2 teaspoons milk, then arrange on a cooky sheet. Sprinkle with coarse salt (Kosher salt, available in Jewish grocery stores, is excellent) and with caraway seed. Bake in a moderate oven (350°) until brown—10 to 12 minutes. Makes about 2½ dozen.

To make salt sticks from roll dough, roll dough very thin (about ⅛ inch) and cut into 3-inch squares. Starting at a corner, roll diagonally to the opposite corner. Brush with egg and sprinkle with salt and caraway as above. Let rise in a warm place until almost double in bulk, and bake in a hot oven (425°) until brown, about 15 minutes.

Mozzarella in Carroza

Literally translated, this is "Mozzarella in a carriage." It is a delicious Italian fried cheese sandwich, which makes a good luncheon dish or snack. Cut into small squares, it can be served as an appetizer. To vary the sandwiches, add small pieces of anchovy fillets or basil leaves to the filling, or flavor the cooking oil with a little fresh garlic.

Make sandwiches of thinly-sliced bread, preferably Italian or French, and Mozzarella cheese, sliced ¼-inch thick. For each 3 full-sized sandwiches, beat 2 eggs with a pinch of salt and a soupçon of pepper. Trim the crusts, cut sandwiches in neat pieces, and soak in the egg for at least 20 minutes, turning once to moisten both sides. Press edges firmly together and sauté in half olive oil, half butter, until nicely browned on both sides. Serve at once.

French Bread Flutes

European travelers are invariably delighted with the long slender loaves of bread that are served in French restaurants and are baked by most small-town *boulangers*. Reasonable facsimiles of these so-called "flutes" are easily made at home.

- 2 packages yeast, active dry or compressed
- 1 cup warm water (lukewarm for compressed yeast)
- 1 ½ teaspoons salt
- 1 tablespoon melted butter
- 3 ½ cups flour (hard wheat flour, available in most health food stores, is best)

Dissolve yeast in warm water. Add salt, melted butter, and 1 cup of the flour. Beat well, then work in the remaining 2 ½ cups flour, and knead until smooth and elastic. Cover and let rise in a warm place until double in bulk. Punch down and let rise a second time.

Turn out on a very lightly floured board and divide into 3 parts. Roll each piece under the palms and fingers to form a long loaf, ¾ inch to 1 inch in diameter. (Twenty inches is the right length for the flute, but make sure it will fit in your pan. If you don't have a pan that is long enough, put two open-end cooky sheets together, or fashion a pan with several layers of heavy foil.)

Put the loaves on the lightly greased pan and, using a razor blade, make diagonal slashes along their full length. Brush with cold water and allow to rise until double in bulk. (The extra amount of yeast will help form bubbles which will bake into holes, a desirable characteristic of French bread.) Brush again with cold water, then bake in a hot oven (425°) for 10 minutes; reduce heat to 350° and bake another 10 minutes or until nicely browned. Makes three 20-inch loaves.

Lucia Buns

In Scandinavian countries a charming custom is observed on December 13, Santa Lucia Day. Young girls, dressed in white robes and wearing wreaths with lighted candles, serve early morning coffee and *lussekake*, or Lucia Buns, to family and friends.

- 2 packages yeast, active dry or compressed
- ¼ cup warm water (lukewarm for compressed yeast)
- 1 cup milk
- ½ cup sugar
- ¾ cup butter or margarine
- 1½ teaspoons salt
- ⅛ teaspoon powdered saffron dissolved in 1 tablespoon water
- 6 cups flour (about)
- Raisins
- Beaten egg
- Sugar

Dissolve yeast in the warm water. Scald milk; add sugar, butter, salt, and saffron. Mix well, cool to lukewarm, then add yeast. Stir in flour and knead lightly; if necessary, add more flour to make the dough easy to handle. Cover and allow to rise until almost double in bulk. Punch down, turn out on a floured board, and knead lightly again. Break off pieces the size of small plums (1¾ inches in diameter), and roll each under the fingers until you have a small rope about 12 inches long. Coil ends in opposite directions, making an "S" with a long body. Cross two of these pieces, so that you have a sort of swastika with curly ends, then put a raisin in the center of each coil and where the two pieces cross.

Allow to rise on a greased baking sheet. Brush with beaten egg, sprinkle with sugar, and bake in a hot oven (400°) for 10 minutes. Reduce heat to moderate (350°), and continue baking for 10 minutes longer, or until nicely browned. Makes about 24 buns.

Watercress and Cheese Sandwiches

If you need a new sandwich filling for tea or for picnics, try this one.

Combine ½ cup finely minced watercress, 1 small package (3 oz.) cream cheese, ½ cup chopped walnuts, and 2 hard-cooked eggs, chopped very fine. Mix well and add salt to taste. Spread between buttered slices of bread. Makes 6 full-sized sandwiches.

Croque Monsieur

The French get the credit for Croque Monsieur, the wonderful snack that is French toast filled like a sandwich.

Assemble sandwiches of sliced ham and sliced Swiss cheese. Trim crusts and press the sandwiches firmly together. Dip in a mixture of 1 slightly beaten egg, a pinch of salt, and ¼ cup of milk. (Mixture is enough for 2 sandwiches. They should be well saturated.) Sauté in butter on both sides until nicely colored. Cut sandwiches in half and serve them piping hot.

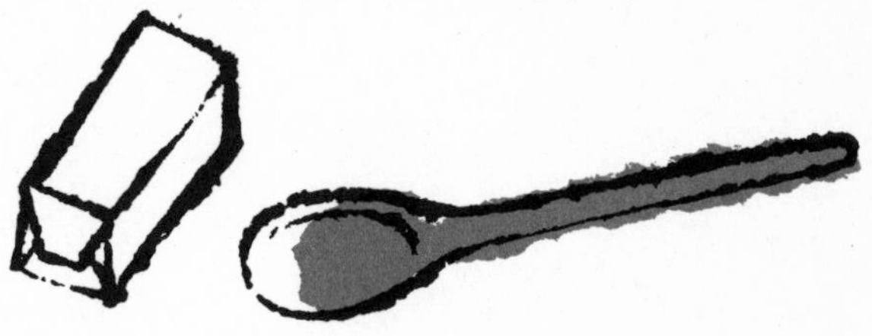

Food cooked en brochette, as you very likely know, means food strung on skewers or small spits and cooked. A broche is a large spit, the one you use for roasting. Next time you remove a roast from the spit for carving, spear your bread on the spit and let it heat while it turns over the coals. Slice a French loaf, spread each slice with butter, garlic butter, onion butter, or soft cheese, and reassemble the loaf; then spear it lengthwise. When the bread is hot, serve it from the spit, letting each person pull off a slice.

Chicken Sandwich De Luxe

Here's an unusual combination that's especially good with tea.

- 1 cup chopped cooked chicken
- ¼ cup crisp crumbled bacon
- ¼ cup chopped filberts
- ½ cup finely cut dates
- Mayonnaise
- Salt to taste
- 12 thin slices buttered bread

Combine chicken, bacon, filberts, dates, and enough mayonnaise to moisten. Add salt, if necessary, and spread on bread slices. Trim crusts and cut in triangles. Makes about 12 full-sized sandwiches or 48 tea-sized ones.

Herb Toast

An herb toast that is good to serve with soup or salad is made with sliced French rolls.

Toast slices on one side. On the other side, spread herb butter made by creaming ¼ pound soft butter with 1 very small pressed clove of garlic, ½ teaspoon lemon juice, and 1 teaspoon each finely chopped chives, parsley, and tarragon. Brown under the broiler.

Open-face Salmon Sandwich

This sandwich makes a hearty lunch or supper, and it's popular with most men. Potato salad goes well with it.

Allow 2 large slices of rye bread for each sandwich. Spread 1 slice with soft butter, and top it with several thin slices of smoked salmon. Spread the other with cream cheese and top with paper-thin slices of raw sweet onion. You can serve each slice open-face or put the slices together and toast each side. Butter the top of each toasted sandwich, cut in diagonal halves, and serve.

Crab and Bacon Open-face Sandwich

Fresh crab meat, crisp bacon, and avocado slices make a wonderful combination of flavors and textures.

Split a long loaf of French bread and spread cut surfaces generously with mayonnaise. Top with 1 pound fresh crab meat, sprinkle with freshly ground black pepper and salt to taste, then top with 1 pound bacon, cooked until crisp and drained. Cut each half of the loaf in two pieces for 4 generous meal-sized servings, or smaller pieces if you want just a snack, and garnish each sandwich with sliced avocado.

Desserts Cakes & Cookies

"I never touch desserts" is a phrase heard often in this weight-conscious world of ours. But few, no matter how vehement they are in their denials, can resist a really delectable one—a luscious, rich, flamboyant dessert that proudly flaunts its calories and dares anyone to turn it down. Hostesses find that men, in particular, love rich desserts, and shamelessly accept second helpings. They may have to make up for it the next day by subsisting on clear soup and raw celery, but they obviously think it's worth it.

A dessert, in some parts of the world, means simply fruit, and although we admit that fruit makes a wonderful finale to a meal, and have included some delicious fruit desserts here, we also include puddings, creams, cakes, fritters, pastries, and soufflés in this category—those delectable dishes which the English so aptly call, simply, "Sweets," and which top off a meal with a special, elegant touch. Some of the desserts in this chapter are fancy enough to have come from a French *patisserie*. Others are simpler, but still distinctive enough to serve as party fare. All, we think, are fun to make, for *that* is the idea of all the recipes in this book.

Apples à la Jacquerie

This dessert is a delightful version of the ever-popular apple dumpling.

Peel tart cooking apples and remove cores. Roll rich pastry ¼ inch thick or a little thicker, and cut into 6 or 7-inch squares (according to the size of the apples). Place an apple on each square, fill centers with apricot jam, brush apples with melted butter, and sprinkle with sugar. (For 5 or 6 apples, you'll need 1 recipe for pastry based on 2 cups flour, and about ⅓ cup apricot jam.)

Bring corners of pastry up over apples and press edges together. Dampen tops and "paste" on a little round of pastry where the four corners meet. Brush all with a slightly beaten egg, and bake in a hot oven (400°) for 5 minutes. Reduce heat to 325° and bake for 30 minutes, or until the crust is brown and the apples tender when pierced through the crust with a pick or skewer. Serve warm, with or without cream.

Baked Apples with Ginger

Serve these apples warm but have cold, heavy cream to pour over them at the table.

Core 6 large baking apples almost to the bottom, and peel halfway down. Mix 1 cup chopped candied or preserved ginger with 1 cup chopped filberts or almonds. Fill cavities with this mixture; put in a baking dish.

Combine 1 cup water, 1 cup sugar, and a 6-ounce glass of currant jelly, and pour into the dish. Bake in a moderate oven (350°) for about 45 minutes, basting occasionally with the syrup in the pan. Sprinkle the apples with granulated sugar and put under the broiler until brown. Makes 6 servings.

Figs Chantilly

This is one of the nicest possible ways to serve fresh figs.

Select fine ripe figs. Make a syrup with equal parts water and sugar. Simmer 5 minutes, then add the figs and cook them for 4 or 5 minutes. Cool in the syrup. Serve with whipped cream flavored with sugar and a little rum flavoring or vanilla.

Fruit Croûtes

Fruit croûtes, a simple French dessert, may be made from puréed fresh fruit. This is a good way to use any fruits that are ripening too quickly.

Slice dry cake (or bread) ½ inch thick, and cut in pieces about 2 by 3 inches. Sauté in butter or margarine on both sides until golden. Spread each slice with apricot, peach, or berry jam, and heap with hot cooked fruit that has been forced through a sieve or whirled in a blender and sweetened to taste. Serve warm with whipped cream or sour cream.

Have you ever wondered why that cherry purloined from the market, that apricot plucked from the tree, or that tomato fresh from the vine tastes so much better than its mate that had a sojourn in the refrigerator? We believe that our passion for "serving cold things cold and hot things hot" may have been overdone. We are convinced that some fruits, like cheese and some wines, should be brought to room temperature before they are eaten.

Winter Fruit Dessert

Oranges and apples are available in the winter when other fresh fruits are often hard to come by. French cooks make a *macedoine* of peeled sliced oranges, apples, and bananas, adding sugar and some liqueur, often kirsch, to taste. Italians use Marsala wine, and omit the bananas.

Core and slice apples, but do not peel them. Peel oranges deeply to remove the white membrane, slice, and remove the seeds. Arrange fruits in layers in a deep glass dish and sprinkle each layer with a little powdered sugar. Pour a generous amount of liqueur or Marsala wine (or sweet sherry) over all, and chill 3 or 4 hours before serving.

Bangkok Banana Fritters

Here's a favorite dessert as it's prepared in Thailand, with coconut and crisp rice. The rice is a specially treated kind that is not available in this country. Instead, we have substituted crisp rice cereal, which works beautifully.

Prepare a batter by mixing 1 cup flour, 2 tablespoons salad oil, 1 cup water, 1 teaspoon baking powder, and ½ teaspoon salt. Set aside. Slightly crush 2 cups crisp rice cereal, using a rolling pin. Combine with 1 cup packaged grated coconut.

Peel 6 ripe bananas, cut in halves crosswise, and scrape outsides. Roll firmly in the coconut-cereal mixture, making sure the sides and ends are thoroughly coated. Heat deep fat to 360°. Dip bananas in the batter, then fry until nicely browned. Do two or three at a time so they won't be crowded. Keep warm in a low oven while the remainder are being fried. Sprinkle with powdered sugar before serving. Makes 12 fritters.

(The Thai cooks also sprinkle drops of the batter into the hot fat, using their fingertips. These brown crisp globules are lifted from the fat with a strainer and sprinkled on top of the fritters before serving.)

Dessert Bananas

This dessert is simple but delicious. You can flame it, if you wish, to make it more festive.

Peel and split 8 bananas, and arrange half of them in a layer in a buttered baking dish. Dot each banana half with 1 teaspoon butter, and sprinkle with cinnamon and sugar (½ tablespoon cinnamon and ½ cup sugar for 8 bananas); add another layer of bananas and repeat butter and sugar routine. Combine ½ cup orange juice and ¼ cup curaçao, and pour over all. Bake in a moderate oven (350°) for 20 minutes, and serve warm. Flame, if you wish, or pass whipped cream. Makes 8 servings.

Pudin de Naranjas

This orange-flavored caramel custard comes from South America. It's a fine ending for a Spanish or Mexican meal.

½ cup sugar
1 ½ tablespoons butter
¾ cup sugar
¼ cup flour
6 eggs, separated
Salt
1 ¼ cups orange juice
1 tablespoon lemon juice

Melt the ½ cup sugar and cook until it turns a lovely amber color. Pour quickly into a 2-quart cold fireproof dish or bowl. Tip quickly so that the sugar forms an even coat on bottom and sides; chill. Cream butter with the ¾ cup sugar, add flour, and mix well. Add a few grains of salt to egg yolks and beat well; combine with orange juice, lemon juice, and the other mixture. Blend well, then fold in the egg whites, beaten stiff. Pour into the caramel-lined bowl, place in a pan of hot water, and bake in a moderate oven (350°) for about 1 hour. Cool slightly and unmold on a serving dish. Serve with curaçao, if desired. Makes 6 servings.

Date Fritters

Date fritters make an unusual dessert.

Remove the pits from ½ pound of dates (about 24), and stuff with the nuts of your choice. Let marinate in sherry or brandy for an hour, then drain. Dip in a fritter batter made by beating together ⅔ cup milk, 1 egg, 1 cup flour, 1 teaspoon sugar, ¼ teaspoon salt, and 2 teaspoons melted butter. Fry, 2 or 3 at a time, in deep fat at 370° until brown. Drain well, and serve with lemon juice. Makes 6 servings.

Profiterolles au Chocolat

This dessert is elegant and impressive, and easy to make.

Make very small cream puff shells, about 1 ½ inches in diameter. Cool, fill with whipped cream, pile in one large pyramid or small individual ones. Over the pyramids pour hot chocolate sauce. (The canned sauce does nicely.)

Flaky Cream Cheese Pastry

Whether you're blessed with a "touch for pastry" or not, you'll find that this recipe comes out rich, tender, and flaky.

Combine 2 small packages (3 oz. each) cream cheese, ½ pound butter, 2 cups flour, and ½ teaspoon salt. Mix together with your hands or an electric mixer until completely blended. Form into a ball, wrap in waxed paper, and chill before using—for pies, tarts, or whenever a particularly rich and delicious pastry is wanted.

Quick Pastries

Every time you have a few scraps of pie crust left, roll it thin and cut it in 4 or 5-inch rounds. Bake and store in the freezer until you have enough for this emergency dessert.

Allow 3 rounds for each serving. Spread one with strawberry jam, top with another round and spread with apricot jam, flavored with Jamaica rum. Add the last round, cover with whipped cream, and sprinkle with darkly toasted slivered almonds.

Gateau Moka

Here's a rich dessert that's made with the homemade ladyfingers on page 185.

- ½ pound soft butter
- 4 egg yolks
- 1½ to 2 cups powdered sugar (½ of a 1-pound package)
- ¼ cup very strong coffee (at least triple-strength)
- About 28 ladyfingers
- Flavored whipped cream (optional)

Make butter cream filling: Cream butter, then gradually beat in egg yolks, powdered sugar, and the coffee. Beat until smooth, thick, and fluffy. Arrange a layer of about 7 whole ladyfingers in a loaf pan (5 by 9 inches); spread with about ¼ of the butter cream. Continue layering the ladyfingers and butter cream, making 4 layers and ending with butter cream. Chill. Slice to serve, topping, if you wish, with whipped cream lightly flavored with rum, Kahlúa, or cognac before slicing. Makes about 10 servings.

Pears Cardinal

This is a rather special dessert that can be fixed in a jiffy.

Chill 1 can (1 lb.) pear halves; drain. Sieve 1 cup ripe strawberries, or put them in a blender (frozen strawberries may be used). Sweeten to taste and pour over the pears, which you have arranged, cut side down, in a shallow dish (or in individual dishes). Stick slivered toasted almonds in the pears, or sprinkle them over the top. Serve with sweetened whipped cream. Makes 4 servings.

Rum Pastry Roses

These are dainty and amusing, and fun to make.

- 1 egg yolk
- 2 whole eggs
- 3 tablespoons powdered sugar
- 1 tablespoon soft butter
- ½ teaspoon salt
- 1 tablespoon Jamaica rum
- 1 cup sifted flour
- Powdered sugar
- Red preserves or jelly

Combine egg yolk and whole eggs, and beat with powdered sugar until light. Mix in butter, salt, rum, and flour. Mix well, turn out on a floured board and knead lightly until smooth. Chill for 15 minutes; divide dough into 4 pieces. Roll, 1 piece at a time, as thin as possible (keep remaining dough cold).

Cut in circles, cutting twice as many with a 1½-inch cutter as with a 1-inch cutter. (Use larger cutters if you want individual desserts.) Stack 2 of the larger pieces together, top with a smaller circle, and press the center, using a small (⅜-inch) cork, the blunt end of a knitting needle, a small dowel, or any similar object. Slash edges of circles with a sharp knife or slit with scissors, to make petals. (Try 8 slashes in the bottom round, 6 in the middle one, and 5 in the top—or do it your own way.) Fry in deep fat at 375° until nicely browned. Be sure to turn them so they color evenly. Drain on paper toweling. Before serving, dust with powdered sugar and put a tiny dab of red preserves or jelly in the center of each full-blown rose. Makes about 40.

Filbert Chocolate Cream Roll

This is one of those fabulously rich desserts that will make everyone forget calories, at least until tomorrow.

- 6 eggs, separated
- ¾ cup sugar
- 1½ cups (lightly packed) grated, unblanched filberts (they may be whirled in a blender)
- ¼ teaspoon salt
- 1 teaspoon baking powder
- Chocolate Butter Cream (below)

Butter a jelly roll pan (about 10 by 15 inches), line it with waxed paper, and butter the paper. Separate eggs, and beat yolks with sugar until thick and light. Combine filberts, salt, and baking powder; fold into the yolk mixture. Beat egg whites until stiff but not dry, and fold into the mixture. Spread in the pan and bake in a moderate oven (350°) for 20 to 25 minutes. Cover with a clean towel that has been wrung out in water, and cool thoroughly. Turn out on the towel, peel off paper, and trim the crisp edges. Spread with Chocolate Butter Cream, and roll like a jelly roll. Chill in refrigerator until serving time.

Chocolate Butter Cream: Combine ¼ cup water, a pinch of cream of tartar, and ¾ cup sugar in a small heavy saucepan. Bring rapidly to a boil and continue boiling until mixture spins a fine thread when a fork is dipped into it and lifted (about 232° on the candy thermometer). Beat 5 egg yolks well; slowly but continually add syrup to yolks, continuing to beat until thick. (Be careful not to pour the syrup into the beater; if you do, the bowl will be lined with sugar threads.) Add 1 cup (½ pound) soft sweet butter; beat until all is smooth and thick. Melt 3 ounces semi-sweet chocolate over hot, not boiling, water. Add to the egg and butter mixture and combine thoroughly. Makes 10 servings.

Maple Mousse

Maple sugar flavors this delightful dessert.

Bring 1 cup pure maple syrup to a boil in the top of a double boiler. Quickly add the well-beaten yolks of 4 eggs and put over boiling water. Whip and cook until thick, about 10 minutes. Cool. Beat the 4 egg whites until stiff, and whip 1 pint of cream. Fold both into the maple mixture, and pour into a 2-quart mold, or into ice cube trays; cover. Freeze. Makes 8 to 12 servings.

Pear Pie

When fresh pears are in season, try them in this delicious pear pie.

Line a pie pan with rich pastry. Peel and slice 6 firm but ripe pears and arrange in layers, sprinkling each layer with cinnamon and sugar. (You will need about ¾ cup sugar, 2 teaspoons cinnamon.) Top with crust, crimp edges prettily, cut a hole in the middle, and glaze with slightly beaten egg. Bake in a hot oven (400°) for about 45 minutes, or until brown. When pie is cool, put a funnel in the hole on top; pour in a mixture of ½ cup heavy cream and 2 tablespoons rum. Serve warm or cold.

In Copenhagen, in the restaurant famous for its 4-foot list of smörrebrød, or open-faced sandwiches, there is one dessert specialty: thin French pancakes, or crêpes, folded around a scoop of vanilla ice cream, and served either plain or with chocolate sauce. It's certainly easy—and even easier if you use a pancake mix.

Strawberries Alexandria

This elaborate-looking dessert is very simple to make. In lieu of the fresh pineapple, you can use 1 large can (1 lb., 14 oz.) sliced pineapple, if you wish.

Cut a ripe pineapple into ½-inch-thick slices; peel. Halve the 4 center slices and cover with 2 tablespoons cognac. Cut the remaining pineapple in dice. Wash 2 baskets strawberries and reserve a dozen of the best ones. Halve the remaining ones and combine with the diced pineapple. Add sugar to taste. Chill. Melt 1 cup apricot preserves; force through a wire strainer, and add 2 tablespoons cognac. Chill. To serve, arrange diced fruits in a mound in the center of a round dish. Surround with the halved pineapple slices, rounded side out. Pour the apricot mixture over all. Cover the center fruits with 1 cup cream, whipped and sweetened to taste. Garnish with the whole strawberries. Makes 6 to 8 servings.

Crème au Chocolat

Serve this rich dessert in small portions, with a plain cooky, ladyfinger, or slice of pound cake, if you wish.

- 1 large package (12 oz.) semi-sweet chocolate pieces
- ¼ cup strong coffee
- Salt
- 2 eggs, separated
- 2 to 4 tablespoons Jamaica rum
- 2 tablespoons sugar
- ½ pint (1 cup) heavy cream

Put chocolate chips in top of a double boiler with the coffee. Bring water in the bottom to a boil, remove from heat, and stir chocolate until it is melted and smooth. Add a pinch of salt and whip in the egg yolks and rum. Let cool. Beat egg whites until they form soft peaks. Gradually beat in sugar, beating until stiff; fold into chocolate mixture. Using the same bowl, whip cream until stiff, add to chocolate, and mix gently until blended. Divide among 10 to 12 small dishes or cups and chill for at least 2 hours before serving. Makes 10 to 12 servings.

Beignets Soufflés

These very light French desserts are like tiny cream puffs but are deep-fried like fritters.

Put ¼ pound butter in a pan with 1 cup water. Stir until the butter is melted, then add ¼ teaspoon salt and 2 teaspoons sugar. Bring to a boil and add 1 cup sifted flour, all at once. Stir vigorously over the heat until a ball forms in the middle of the pan. Cool slightly, then beat in 1 whole egg. When thoroughly incorporated, add another, then a third. If the eggs are large, this will suffice; if small, add a fourth. The dough should be shiny and yellow, but not too soft.

Drop teaspoonfuls of the dough in deep fat at 360° until puffed and brown. Sprinkle with sugar before serving. These can also be filled, if you wish, with whipped cream, custard, or preserves, or served with a liqueur-flavored fruit sauce. Makes 3 to 4 dozen small puffs.

Chocolate Rum Mousse

Here's a different kind of chocolate mousse, made with sour cream and macaroons.

Melt ½ cup semi-sweet chocolate pieces. Add 1 cup sour cream, ⅓ cup powdered sugar, a pinch of salt, 1 tablespoon rum, and 1 cup of crumbled macaroons. Put in an ice cube tray or in individual paper cases and freeze. Makes 6 servings.

Macaroon Peaches

You can use canned peach halves for this delicious dessert, but first you must have macaroons—large enough to make a base for the peaches. The homemade ones on page 186 are ideal.

Put a peach half—either fresh (peeled) or canned—on a macaroon, and pour over a syrup made by whirling 1 package frozen raspberries in the blender (or forcing them through a sieve), and flavoring it with 2 tablespoons Framboise (or cognac or kirsch).

Chantilly Parfait

Crème Chantilly, as you probably know, is nothing more than sweetened whipped cream. Chantilly parfait has egg whites added and is frozen. It couldn't be easier.

Add 1 tablespoon water to 2 egg whites and beat stiff but not dry. Beat in ½ cup powdered sugar and add a few grains of salt and 1 teaspoon vanilla. Fold in 1 cup heavy cream, beaten thick but not stiff. Freeze in ice trays and serve in parfait glasses, with preserved fruit or sweetened fresh fruit at the bottom and a garnish of whipped cream or chopped nuts on top. Makes 6 servings.

Double-boiler Soufflé

This is an old and infallible recipe for a dessert soufflé that's made in a double boiler.

Separate 6 eggs and beat the whites until stiff but not dry. Beat in ⅓ cup sugar and a few grains of salt. Fold in ⅓ cup bitter orange marmalade, and pour into the well-greased top of a double boiler. Cover and put over boiling water. Steam for 1 hour. If dinner is delayed, let the soufflé stand over hot water, but don't remove cover.

While the soufflé is cooking, make a sauce with the 6 egg yolks beaten with ¼ cup sugar. Add to 1½ cups hot milk, and cook, stirring, until thick. Don't allow to boil. Add 3 or 4 tablespoons Jamaica rum, or rum flavoring to taste. Turn soufflé out on a warm dish and pour the sauce around it. Makes 6 servings.

Tarte aux Framboise

This is a lovely dessert for a summer meal.

Make the French type of pastry called pâté brisée: Sift 1 cup all-purpose flour onto a pastry board. Drop 1 egg yolk, 1 tablespoon sugar, ½ cup soft butter, 1 teaspoon grated lemon peel, and ¼ teaspoon salt in a well made in the middle of the flour, and mix to a smooth dough. If dough is too stiff, add a few drops of ice water. Press dough into a 9-inch pie pan, fluting the edges of the dough. Chill for 1 hour.

Fill the shell with heavy aluminum foil cut in a large circle and pleated at the sides to fit perfectly inside the shell. Bake in a moderate oven (350°) for 30 minutes, or until brown. Cool, remove foil, and fill with fresh raspberries (you'll need about 1 pint of berries). Melt 1 cup raspberry jelly, pour over the berries, and cool. Serve with or without whipped cream.

Ricotta Pie

This is called *torta di Ricotta* in Italy, and is an Italian version of cheese cake.

2 cups flour
⅔ cup butter, or butter and shortening
2 tablespoons Marsala or sherry wine
1 small egg
½ teaspoon salt
Water (if needed)
1½ pounds Ricotta cheese
¼ cup sugar
½ cup semi-sweet chocolate pieces, chopped coarsely
1 teaspoon vanilla or almond extract
1 teaspoon grated orange peel
4 eggs, well beaten
Blanched almonds or filbert halves

First make the pastry: Combine flour, butter, wine, the 1 egg, salt, and, if needed, a few drops of water. Roll thin and line a 10-inch pie pan with part of the pastry, reserving remaining pastry.

Beat or blend Ricotta cheese until smooth; add sugar, chocolate pieces, vanilla, orange peel, and the 4 beaten eggs. Fill the pastry shell, cut remaining pastry in strips, and criss-cross over the top. Put a blanched almond or filbert half in each open square, and bake in a moderately hot oven (375°) for 45 minutes, or until the pastry is nicely browned. Cool slowly. Makes 6 to 8 servings.

Sabayon

This is the French version of zabaglione. It's made with cognac instead of Marsala wine.

Beat 6 egg yolks with 6 tablespoons sugar and a few grains of salt until thick. Put in the top of a double boiler over hot (not boiling) water, add ¼ cup cognac, and cook, beating with a whisk, until thick. Take care not to overcook or it will curdle. Pour into warmed sherbet glasses and serve warm. Makes 6 small servings.

Ladyfingers

Many classic desserts call for ladyfingers, but good ones are not easy to find. They are easy to make, however, and freeze beautifully. The same batter can be used for sponge drops (below) which make nice *petits fours* when put together with a butter cream filling (your own recipe or the one on page 178).

Sift flour, measure ¾ cup plus 1 tablespoon, and sift again with ⅓ cup sugar and a dash of salt; sift again. Separate 4 eggs and beat the whites stiff, gradually beating in ⅓ cup sugar. Beat the yolks until thick and lemon-colored, adding 1 teaspoon vanilla; fold into the beaten whites. Sift the sugar and flour mixture over eggs; fold in carefully.

Fill 24 greased ladyfinger pans, or, using a plain tube and a pastry bag, pipe the batter onto cooky sheets that have been greased and lightly dusted with cornstarch, forming fingers about 4 inches long and slightly narrower in the middle than on the ends. (They will spread slightly in cooking; when baked they should be about 4½ inches long, 1 inch wide in the center, and 1¼ inches wide at the ends.) Bake in a moderate oven (350°) for 13 minutes, or until lightly browned. Cool slightly before removing from the pans. Makes 4 to 5 dozen.

To make sponge drops, drop batter by the half-teaspoonful (or make dots with the pastry bag) onto cooky sheets prepared as above. Bake in a moderate oven (350°) for 10 to 12 minutes, and cool as above.

Pots de Crème Vanille

Ceramic *petits pots*, little pots with covers, are the traditional serving dish for this dessert.

Beat 6 egg yolks until thick and light, then beat in a pinch of salt, ½ cup fine granulated sugar, and 1½ teaspoons vanilla. Scald 2 cups heavy cream, beat a little of it into the mixture, then combine with the remaining cream. Strain into the pots, cover, and put into a baking pan. Add enough hot water to come within half an inch of the tops of the pots. Bake in a moderate oven (350°) for 40 to 45 minutes, or until a table knife comes out clean. Chill. Makes 6 servings.

Lemon Meringue Bars

This rather rich cooky, good with tea (iced or hot) or with ice cream, is not difficult to make.

½ cup (¼ pound) butter
½ cup powdered sugar
2 egg yolks
1 cup sifted flour
¼ teaspoon salt
2 teaspoons grated lemon peel
2 egg whites
½ cup granulated sugar
1 tablespoon lemon juice

Put together in a bowl the butter, powdered sugar, egg yolks, flour, salt, and lemon peel. Knead with the hands until the mixture is smooth and the color evenly distributed. Spread in a 10-inch square or 10 by 12-inch ungreased pan, and bake in a moderate oven (350°) for 10 minutes. Remove from oven and allow to cool while making meringue. Beat egg whites until stiff. Add sugar gradually. Add lemon juice, and beat until the meringue stands in peaks. Spread meringue on cooky dough and return to the oven for 20 to 25 minutes, or until nicely browned. Cool and cut into bars. Makes about 2 dozen.

Macaroons

Homemade macaroons are delicious alone, or as a base for other delightful desserts.

Get some almond paste at a fancy grocer or from a bakery—¼ pound will suffice. Knead it with your hands until soft. Put an unbeaten egg white in a bowl with a pinch of salt; start to beat it, adding ½ cup finely granulated sugar and the almond paste, a little at a time. Continue beating until all is used and the mixture is smooth and just thick enough to hold its shape for a few seconds. (If not thick enough, add a little powdered sugar.)

Butter a baking pan and dust with cornstarch. Drop the macaroon batter on in heaping tablespoonfuls, leaving plenty of space between them, as they should spread out. Bake in a slow oven (300°) until slightly tinged with brown, about 25 minutes. Let stand for a minute before removing from the pan with a spatula. Makes about 9 macaroons, each about 2 inches in diameter.

Coriander Cookies

Coriander and cardamom flavor this attractive cooky. It's as good to eat as it is good looking. If you can't find ground coriander, grind the whole seed with a mortar and pestle or in an electric blender. These freeze nicely.

3 eggs
¾ cup soft butter
2 ½ cups sugar
3 ½ cups sifted flour
1 tablespoon baking powder
½ teaspoon salt
2 teaspoons ground coriander
1 teaspoon ground cardamom
Grated peel of 1 lemon
Currant jelly or strained apricot jam
½ cup finely minced almonds

Beat 2 of the eggs with the butter and 1 ½ cups of the sugar until light. Mix in flour, baking powder, salt, coriander, cardamom, and lemon peel. Mix thoroughly, then refrigerate for 1 hour. Turn out on a floured board; roll ½ inch thick and cut in strips 1 ½ inches wide. Using a ½-inch dowel or the handle of a wooden spoon, press a groove down the middle of each strip. Transfer to greased cooky sheets and pipe a strip of currant jelly or strained apricot jam into the groove, using a pastry tube (or carefully spoon in the jelly).

Bake in a moderate oven (375°) for 15 minutes. Remove from oven, brush with the remaining 1 egg that has been beaten with the remaining ½ cup sugar. Sprinkle with almonds, and return to oven for 5 minutes. Cut into 1 ½-inch diagonal bars. Makes about 4 dozen.

Date Bars

These are easy to make and well liked by almost everyone.

Sift flour, measure out 1 cup, then sift again with 1 teaspoon each baking powder and salt. Mix in 2 cups dark brown sugar, 2 well-beaten eggs, and 1 teaspoon vanilla. Add 1 cup pitted dates, cut in pieces with scissors, and ½ cup coarsely chopped walnut meats; mix well. Grease a 7 ½ by 11 ½-inch pan and line it with waxed paper; spread with cooky mixture, and bake in a moderate oven (350°) for 20 minutes, or until nicely browned. Cool slightly, turn out of pan, peel off paper, and cut into bars. Makes about 2 dozen.

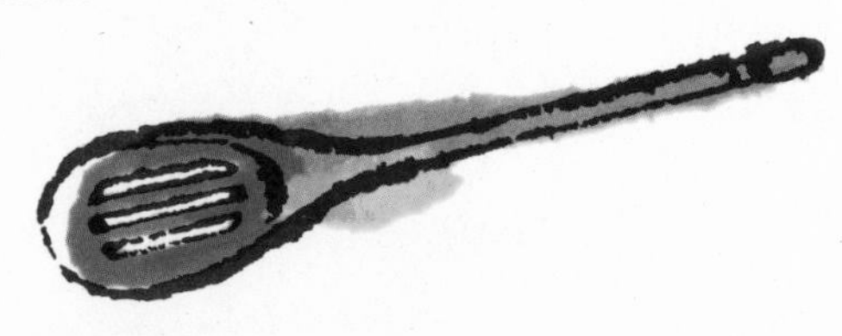

Index

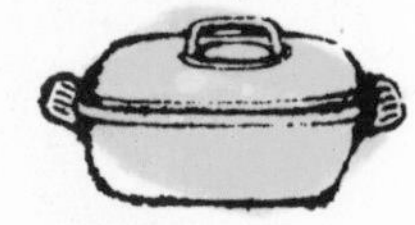

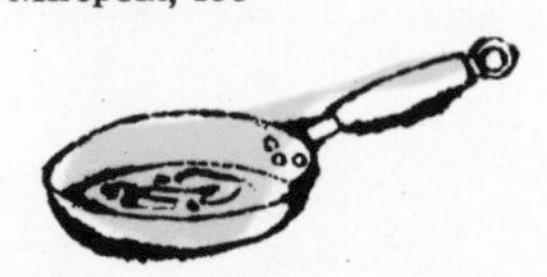

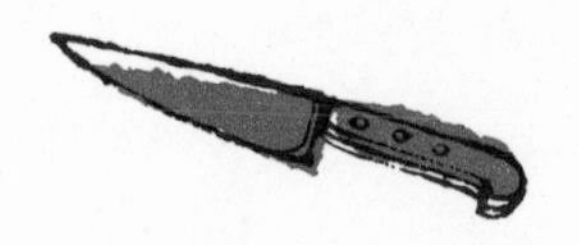